When the

Pastor

is your *Husband*

When the
Pastor
is your *Husband*

THE JOY AND PAIN OF MINISTRY WIVES

BY DONNA BORDELON ALDER

BEACON HILL PRESS
OF KANSAS CITY

Copyright 2011
Donna Bordelon Alder and Beacon Hill Press of Kansas City

ISBN 978-0-8341-2722-7

Printed in the
United States of America

Cover Design: Lindsey Rohner
Interior Design: Sharon Page

Library of Congress Cataloging-in-Publication Data

Alder, Donna Bordelon.
    When the pastor is your husband : the joy and pain of ministry wives / by Donna Bordelon Alder.
       p. cm.
    Includes bibliographical references (p.   ).
    ISBN 978-0-8341-2722-7 (pbk.)
    1. Spouses of clergy. 2. Wives. I. Title.
    BV4395.A43 2011
    253'.2—dc23

                                                              2011022589

10 9 8 7 6 5 4 3 2 1

Contents

Acknowledgments

There is a great host of women—and a couple of men—who contributed to this book. Their efforts have surrounded its pages and made it possible. Dr. Linda Hardin read and reread every word and encouraged me repeatedly. My husband, who has been in my grandstand since I have known him, has read and corrected every chapter. Gaye Andre, Jan Werner, and Marcia O'Brien have prayed regularly for its effective ministry. Cheryl Roland, Joyce Williams, Dr. Cecil Paul, Eunice Rayborn of Focus on the Family, and scores of ministry wives have contributed to administering, collecting, or completing the survey used as a basis for its content. Esther Gillie, Lindsey Merchant, Dr. Bonnie Descoteaux, Dr. Cynthia Symons, Karen Scheske, Candie Pocock, Amy Porpilia, and Kerri Todd have added their editing skills or helped collect information or contributed to enlightening me on the statistics of my data. Lorien Urban has done a lion's share of critiquing my thoughts and giving me clarifying advice.

To these I tender my thanks, and may God be glorified and find their work and mine useful in bringing His kingdom to earth.

Introduction

I hope this book will bring advice and encouragement to the tens of thousands of ministry wives who are struggling with the unanticipated challenges of life as a pastor's wife. There is much about the ministry that is delightful, uplifting, rewarding, and motivating, and we will look at those aspects. The facets that are frustrating sometimes need to be drawn from their darker corners and exposed to the light of day, examined, and put into eternal perspective. The finest place to do this is in the company of wise, courageous women who have faced these same facets, gathered the wisdom of their experience and put it into godly advice and counsel. Like good friends whose company is cherished when life is filled with questions, this book is designed to join the ministry wife on her path and stay for a time to help her as she travels. Thousands of women are gathered in the grandstand along the way, ready to encourage each woman and enlighten the steps she is about to take or the ones she has already taken. Many have prayed that this advice and counsel will give her a bright hope in her future as a ministry wife.

ONE

How It Started

For anyone who comes to God must believe that he exists and that he rewards those who search for him. (Hebrews 11:6, NEB)

$\mathcal{I}$ don't know where the venue is for your emotional low points. Maybe it's your bedroom during the dark hours of the night when you fret instead of sleep. Maybe it's in the bathroom on Sunday morning when the confusion and pressure of preparing your family for church is exasperating. Maybe it's in church after a heated argument with your husband as you sit piously and reflect on your unchristian behavior. Maybe your single lowest point is a memory so powerful that its place is an icon to your doubts, your sadness, or your frustrations.

Mine is like that. It is in my basement, in front of my washing machine. It was there that I collected all the discouragements of the week, swept them into a pile, and cast them into the air to settle on all my thoughts and reflections. Gathering and ruminating during that time in my life finally led to a period of doubting that tried the faith of my young adulthood. Perhaps you have not had such dark troughs, but I have. My story is one of doubt, great grace, and powerful providence. To be honest, I am thankful that I had to journey through it. In the end it was the tunnel to the road of a maturing faith. I tell it now to encourage you on your journey.

I stood before my washing machine in the basement of the parsonage and ground my teeth with frustration as I loaded yet *another* batch of dirty diapers into the washing machine. My husband and I had recently moved to a new church, I had delivered a new baby, and the pressing demands of my three small children were overwhelming. The washing machine represented the never-ending tedium that filled my life. I felt as if I had spent more emotional effort doing mindless tasks than I had on the grueling work required for my schooling. I cleaned up after children, changed diapers, slept rarely, washed mountains of clothes, cooked—all the thankless tasks involved in rearing three children five and under. The loss of control over much of my life kept me groping for some handhold in the downward spiral of my thoughts. I recognize now that some of what I suffered was postpartum blues, isolation that comes from being fully occupied with small children, the losses of leaving the routine of one church and trying to settle into another, and an inability to communicate with a husband struggling with his own sense of loss during that transition.

Before many weeks, the physical, emotional, and mental turmoil at the core of my life spilled onto the shores of a young, lightly tested, free-floating faith. The pulling vortex that had begun in my mind, body, and emotions increased as I began questioning my spiritual beliefs. The walls of this whirlpool became more and more slippery, and I could not slow my descent into a darkness that St. John of the Cross describes as the "dark night of the soul."

While I now have a perspective on what God was doing then, what I needed to surrender, what exacerbated the situation, what could have helped, what lessons the dark times taught about God's faithfulness, and what useful purposes the experience served for the benefit of others, I could not recognize God in any of it at the time. Like Lynne Hybels, I found it very inconvenient to lose my faith as a pastor's wife.

And lose it I did. At least it felt that way. I sat in my customary pew at church, looking around the sanctuary and considering the futility of all the mortar and brick, the words from book and hymnal. *What if there really was not an eternal God?* It seemed a considered possibility, and the thought of it left me almost breathless with darkness. *What was the purpose of repeating the empty words and songs? Was there any point to two hundred people coming together except to generate social connections?*

In my darkest hours, the possibility that this faith stuff could be meaningless enveloped me. I continued in the routines of church, shaking hands, smiling, singing in the choir; yet a hollowness of spirit followed me. One Sunday, in quiet frustration, I began a bargaining process with God.

God, if you are there, show me. For weeks I waited. Nothing.

OK, I countered one Sunday, *I'll give a little.*

It seems that arrogance and control were both part of the issue, but my heart was impatient at the darkness of my thoughts. My honest doubts drove me. I continued the bargain. *OK, God, I'll start with belief that you are. Can you work with that bit of faith and show me who you are?*

I waited, considering the pledge. I closed my eyes and repeated my bargaining. *God, you are.* It was a difficult step, but speaking those words marked a beginning. Over the next few weeks I felt confirmed in the thought that if I came to God believing that He was, He would identify himself to me.

After a time I took another step—slowly, honestly, fully expressing my doubts to God.

God, I will choose to believe that you are there and that you will reward my efforts to find you. I am not convinced of this yet, but I will give ground on this subject and begin with that little grain of belief. Now, please, please, confirm these things to me.

Audacious as it seems, it was a contract—an honesty I had not heretofore adopted. As a twenty-something, I had never let myself come to the point of facing my doubts squarely. I kept shoving them into a place where they could not be seen by me or others. I might poke my finger into the darkness, but I had not dragged out the contents and confronted the pile of questions in the light of day. Now, at thirty-something, it would happen because of this pivotal darkness. I pulled out the pile and spread its dark contents onto the dimly lit floor of my soul. This time, however, I invited God to help me consider the pile.

There was no immediate release or settling of faith. But I was satisfied that this was the only way to begin.

While the shadowy questions lay strewn about in my heart, outwardly life appeared normal. I went to church, managed to attend three services a week, and kept home and hearth running. It was a constant chore to continue the apparent normalcy, but I did. Some days I would stop the car before turning onto my street and pause, considering what might happen if I simply drove away to some unknown freedom and not return. In the end, with great effort, I corralled my thoughts and proceeded to the mundane tasks before me.

It seems God had accepted the honest bargain of a weary, empty heart, and He proceeded with it. Slowly He began to mend and reorient my heart. A friend of mine understood that I was going through something very difficult and recommended to the church board that I be given finances to attend a weekend retreat for those in ministry. That weekend was a step in my climb back into God's felt grace. With increasing frequency God revealed His heart of mercy until I no longer questioned, nor have I since doubted the existence and love of my Father. It was a layered process, but building a reasoning, maturing faith is often best accomplished in gradual steps.

One afternoon on my path to recovery, after attending a small group about the disciplines of Christian life, I sensed that I should consider the topic of obedience to the "voice of God," whatever that might look like. The bargaining continued.

OK, God, I'll consider this and try to follow this obedience concept. You know you will need to increase my compliance. It is not something I can do alone.

I collected my two preschoolers from the nursery at the church where the group met and decided to take them to a park for an afternoon of play. I was unfamiliar with my new neighborhood and had no idea where a park might be located. Feeling especially trusting, I reasoned, *I'll try this "God, lead me to a park" thing and see if it works.*

I began turning randomly down the streets of my community and soon came upon a small park attached to an apartment complex. *How delightful for God to direct me to this park,* I thought. Or, maybe it was just coincidence. Hmmm.

The children tumbled out of the car and raced to the swings perched in an open field of green. I settled against a low wooden fence nearby and rejoiced in the warmth of the day. I closed my eyes and let the sun shine on my face.

I sensed God's presence. *There is a woman on the other end of this fence, and she needs your help to hear from me today,* He murmured.

Startled, I opened my eyes, surprised to see a young woman watching a preschooler romp about the play area. She appeared to be in her second trimester of pregnancy.

Jesus, I can't do that. She would probably be offended. This is not something I feel comfortable doing.

He reminded me: *Did we just have a conversation about obedience to the voice of God not ten minutes ago?*

I paused, lingering as I tried to manage some small courage. *Just remember I can't do this on my own. You need to open the door.* I was midway between hoping that the door would not open and wishing I could see God at work, when the lovely auburn-haired woman edged over to my end of the fence.

She began chatting amiably about her son and her life in the apartment complex. I asked about her due date, and she looked at me for a moment. Her eyes lingered on my face, and worry filled them with shadows.

"I am due in four months," she said, then paused. "I just lost a baby a year ago through miscarriage, and I am so afraid this pregnancy will not be successful that I can't sleep." Her lips drew thin with disquiet.

I understood now why God had directed me to this park. This was way past the possibility of happenstance; it was divinely coordinated providence. I listened until I was sure she had expressed all that she needed to before I began.

"Four years ago the same thing happened to me. I lost a son through miscarriage after five months of pregnancy. There was guilt, questions I couldn't answer, and pain in my heart. After a few months I became pregnant again. I lived in anguish like yours, afraid this baby would suffer the same fate as the last one until one morning I talked to God about my fears. I told Him all that was buried under my attempts to be brave. When I was done, I gave my future to Him and left my unborn child in His hands. From that point on I knew that He cared and would be with me. He released me from my fears, and I learned to rest in His love. The happy little boy climbing up the slide over there was the baby that was safely delivered at the end of that pregnancy. But I have God to thank for the peace I experienced during most of that time."

She stared at me and swallowed. Her eyes softened as she brushed her hair back from her cheek in thoughtful silence.

We spent twenty minutes or so in deep conversation. She questioned me, and I answered with what I can only say was God's assurance for her. When we parted I was amazed at the providence of this God I had questioned and deeply doubted not long ago.

In this and many other ways God began to confirm himself to me. I came to cherish the verse in Hebrews that says "he who comes to God must believe that He is, and that He is a rewarder of those who diligently seek Him" (Hebrews 11:6, NKJV). It seemed to explain the process that gave me hope and faith in a loving God.

While in the middle of the darkness, however, I cast about for a book or journal or accessible route to take me back to firm ground, but I could find little that helped answer my questions or gave me support as a pastor's wife. My graduate research had given me practice in the skill of asking questions, gathering and analyzing data, and drawing conclusions. I wondered if God could use any of these proficiencies to help others who experienced what I had. In an effort to determine if other pastors' wives endured this darkness, and if so, what contributed to it, how they coped, what steps resolved it, and what they had learned from it, I developed a questionnaire that I hoped to distribute to other pastors' wives.

My first attempts to find answers were encouraged by Dr. Cecil Paul, a psychology professor. He graciously consented to distribute the questionnaire to another group of pastors' wives in Ohio, and I collected and analyzed the data. He was the first among many who believed in the value of helping pastors' wives through this tool.

The subsequent development, distribution, collection, and analysis of this questionnaire have been aided by a host of wonderful people including the Women's Ministry of the Church of the Nazarene, Focus on the Family, Sheppard's Ministry, the counseling staff and faculty of Roberts Wesleyan College, faculty colleagues from Asbury College and Houghton College, and, most of all, ministry wives around the world. It has been distributed in Kenya and in Hungary and translated into three languages.

As I share the results of the responses I received from women in ministry in the United States, it is my hope that you will find support and comfort from those who have had common experiences. I have also looked at surveys done with diverse ministry wives and have gathered the themes common in these answers so that what is said is supported by the voices of many.

The pastors' wives who completed these questionnaires gave important advice on problems they faced, the ways they have managed difficulties, and the joys that encouraged them. Collectively they have spoken and shared their insights, and you now have the opportunity to hear from all of them.

It is unacceptable that you should ever feel as if there is no hope or that you are alone and cannot find someone to come alongside you. There is help for the challenges you face from veteran pastors' wives who have seen the grace of God sustain them in all manner of circumstances.

■ FOR YOUR CONSIDERATION

1. Can you identify with any of the emotions expressed in this chapter? If so, which ones speak to you?
2. Do you think ministry wives have a more difficult time than most women? If so, why? If not, why not?
3. What do you think this statement means? "It is a terrible thing to waste a crisis."
4. If you have reached a place of overwhelming doubt, discuss this with God even if you question His existence. Read Isaiah 1:18. What do you think it means? Are there some issues that you don't feel comfortable reasoning about with God? Examine these. Can you determine why you feel that way?
5. Both David and Job have written of their conversations with God. Read their exchanges, especially Psalm 88. Can you identify with David's sentiments? Does it seem reasonable to express these feelings to God?

The book of Job, according to William P. Brown, is primarily about Job. It charts his journey through doubt to a new paradigm of faith. Job pulls out many of the hard questions about God that humankind has asked, and in the end God says to Job's friends, "you have not spoken of me what is right, as my servant Job has" (Job 42:7). Brown suggests this means Job's honest questions and feelings were acceptable to God. In James 5:11, Job is commended for his perseverance. When Job thinks to be silent before God and not express his frustration, God tells him to be a man and speak his thoughts (40:6-7).[1]

God says to you, *Come be a woman of courage and speak to me of these things in your heart. It's OK. Tell me all you think and feel.*

Let's take a look at the survey tools used to ensure that the answers given in this book really come from ministry wives in the trenches.

TWO

The Surveys

Without counsel purposes are disappointed: but in the multitude of counsellors they are established. (**Proverbs** 15:22, KJV)

It happened shortly after I began the slow climb into spiritual daylight, at a time when I regularly contemplated my experiences in the dark night of the soul, gazed into my own heart, and still questioned. One Saturday afternoon when I was performing household chores, my husband relayed the chilling news about Jenna (not her real name).

She was one of the most beautiful women I had ever met. Her blue eyes reflected an easy, warm smile. Her lovely toss of bright blond hair curved around her flawless face and neck. She was tall and graceful, and she laughed easily during conversations I had with her at statewide events. For that reason, I felt she must be happy with life. She had a quiet charm that I mistook for a quiet spirit. She had three growing children, and her husband pastored a modest church in a neighboring city. From all appearances, he loved her dearly.

One Sunday, while her children and husband were in church, she committed suicide in the parsonage.

When I heard the news, the muscles in my chest drove the breath from my lungs, and that breathless feeling clung like suffocating mist over my thoughts that day. I was frightened to think someone so lovely and gracious had taken such a step. At that time in my life, I was at home with my children and enduring the tumult of postpartum adjustments, a new church assignment, and an unfamiliar parsonage. The people in our previous church, who had loved us and cared for us for five wonderful years, were far away, and I was just becoming acquainted with our new parishioners. I was lonely and constantly pushed to satisfy the demands of my children without the moorings of extended family, dealing with the unfamiliar, and adjusting to a change in hormonal levels.

Although I was on the ascent from a dark place of my own, it was easy for me to vicariously slide down into her perspective. For months after her funeral that same suffocating mist overtook my thoughts regularly. I cannot say mine were thoughts of self-destruction, but thoughts of escape were still enticing. I called to God, and He enabled me to hang on—but far from triumphantly. Eventually, after a remarkable series of God-ordained events, some of which have been related to you, that mist lifted and has thankfully never returned.

Jenna's experience—and my own—precipitated in me a desire to come alongside pastors' wives who endure such unanticipated dark periods. In response to this, I developed a questionnaire that was eventually distributed to 469 women worldwide.

Over the past fifty years, there have been several ministry wives' surveys, some with strong credentials including random sampling, large sample size, and careful statistical analysis; some with less validated data, convenience sampling, and little analysis. Altogether, they deserve some attention in describing us. In addition to my survey, six other surveys are referred to in an attempt to gain a general picture of ministry wives. Each survey had its own set of unique characteristics; some surveyed only one denomination or area of the United States, some used many denominations, many areas. Together they say something about who we are demographically and what we think about life as ministry wives.

There are several reasons why this look at ourselves is useful. It diminishes unrealistic expectations of who we think we are. That alone should provide some stress relief. It clarifies negative issues, allowing us to see them from a logical whole.

It is my hope that in the following chapters you will see how the troubling aspects of this role are handled successfully by other women.

Below is a capsule summary of each survey, given so that you may reflect on the accuracy and comparison value of each:

- Alder, 2009: 439 ministry wives, eighteen denominations, mainly Church of the Nazarene, all over United States, convenience sampling[1]
- Alleman, 1987: 228 ministry wives, four denominations, mainly California[2]
- Brunette-Hill, 1990: 105 ministry wives, all of United Church of Christ, all in Wisconsin, surveyed all the population[3]
- Crow, 1990: 570 National Evangelical Association ministry wives, random sampling, all over the United States[4]
- Douglas, 1965: 4,777 ministry wives, all Protestant denominations (37), random sampling, all over the United States[5]
- Taylor, 1975: 448 ministry wives, stratified random sampling, six denominations[6]

- Valeriano, 1981: 166 ministry wives, convenience sampling of readers of *Leadership* Journal[7]

The reliability of specific data must be carefully considered and comparisons should be made with some caution. That said, some interesting consistencies emerge:

- **Age of ministry wives.** It seems consistent when comparing all the surveys that the older the survey was, the younger was the average age of the participant.

- **Years of service in ministry.** All the surveys indicated that sixty to eighty percent of these women have been in ministry for ten years or more.

- **Is their role a calling?** Most women did not feel that being a pastor's wife is a calling, but it was commonly felt that it was God's will for them.

- **Feelings about their role.** There is one point made by the surveys that needs to be remembered throughout this book. The great majority of ministry wives feel fulfilled in their role.

- **Education.** Ministry wives are well educated. The more recent the data, the more educated the women.

- **Employment.** Currently about three-fourths of us work outside the home. About one quarter did during the sixties.

- **Feelings about salaries.** Salaries were low and finances place formidable stress on ministry wives, but for the most part they felt they were managing.

- **Marriage.** Ministry wives are generally happy in their marriages.

- **Involvement in ministry.** Most women felt comfortable helping their husbands' ministries in the background or in a supportive manner. They managed five or fewer jobs in the church.

- **Pressure to conform.** Many felt pressure to conform, many did not. Most felt they had the freedom to be themselves.

- **Problems they face.** Several difficulties surfaced when asked what problems they faced or what they would change about ministry. According to the Douglas, Brunette-Hill, Alder, and Valeriano women, the top two were "husband's work schedule" and "lack of friends, or loneliness." Also mentioned was financial pressure, and very high on the list were expectations and critical people.

- **Joys of ministry.** Most enjoyed working beside their husbands, seeing people mature spiritually in their faith, being of service, and learning more about their beliefs. Most felt their families had richly benefited from this role.

- **Discouragement.** Most, but not all of us, have had times of discouragement of varying intensities.

  A little less than half experienced frequent ups and downs or got discouraged occasionally. In my study, twelve percent experienced dysthymia, twenty-two percent experienced depression, and twenty-three percent rarely if ever got discouraged. This last group is statistically older and has been in ministry longer than either of the three previous groups.

- **Description of the ministry wife role.** When asked what words described their role, most in the Crow and Alder studies said "challenging," then "rewarding"/"satisfying." Less than one in five included negative words, such as "hurtful," "frightening," or "the pits." Crow indicates that this assessment changes with the size of the congregation and age of respondent. Generally, the smaller the church and the younger the ministry wife, the more negative the response.

- **What helps with discouragement?** When asked what helped them most with discouragement, in my study the great majority indicated their spiritual life of prayer and Bible reading. In Crow's study about one-third indicated they needed outside help in overcoming discouragement and depression. This last figure correlated with the size of the church.

- **Friends.** Half to three-fourths of the ministry wives surveyed have friends in the church or have felt free to make friends in the church.

In trying to summarize the general picture of ministry wives it becomes clear that there was and is a wide variety of women who fill this role. In every category, it is difficult to generalize or summarize an average characteristic, so be encouraged, there is no mold into which most fit. Young, old, have friends in the church or not, feel free to be themselves or not, feel called or not, experience frequent ups and downs or rarely get discouraged, work outside the home or not—you will find ample company among ministry wives.

There were general themes that clearly settled in this flurry of data. Ministry wives were well educated, generally happy about their positions, had several things they wish were different, but overall were glad they were in this life. As they age, they were increasingly satisfied with what they did and had gained a better view of themselves. They were generally satisfied with their marriages and discovered that the greatest thing going for most of them was spiritual strength derived from Scripture and prayer.

But the general picture of things does not satisfy us when we are striving against discouragement. Wouldn't it be a relief to hear that many other ministry wives have experienced the same downsides, that most have learned what it takes to overcome and successfully move past disappointments that accompany life in the church? It is my hope to let you know that we have been there, we are there, we have seen the illusions implode and the expectations mount, and we have seen God's grace at work when the road seems paved with futility. We have learned many comforting lessons, useful ways of thinking, soul-nurturing, grace-filled healing packets of truth that we will share. There is wisdom to be gained from the hand of God in our sometimes glorious, always challenging lives.

Let's see what makes it glorious.

■ FOR YOUR CONSIDERATION

1. In what ways do you feel you conform to most of the women described here? In what ways are you different?
2. What circumstances do you feel are so unique to you that most people, even other pastors' wives, would not understand?
3. What makes pastors' wives often reluctant to express true feelings about ministry?
4. What have you learned over the course of your life and ministry that you feel would benefit other pastors' wives?
5. Do you find it hard to make friends in church or be yourself most of the time? If so, why do you think that is?

THREE

Remember the Good

Whatever is true, whatever is noble, whatever is right, whatever is pure, whatever is lovely, whatever is admirable . . . think about such things. (Philippians 4:8)

$\mathcal{I}$ stood one winter afternoon with a crowd of people waiting to board a flight to Colorado Springs when I noticed a gregarious, outspoken, gray-haired gentleman who was attempting a conversation with a woman who was only mildly interested in his thoughts. Because flying has become such a bane to me, I hoped he would not be in the seat next to mine so I could be free to hunker down and suffer in personal silence for the duration of the flight. As providence would have it, he glided into the aisle seat one place removed from me.

Hoping to ignore him, I huddled over my book. I am grateful now that my attempts did not impede his inquiries. What we discussed on that flight has remained with me to this day.

I discovered that he was not only a dean in a local seminary, but when he handed me his card, I realized he was blessed with a string of academic letters behind his name that assured me he had credentials: PhD, ThD, MAC, and so forth. Among his qualifications was a graduate degree in counseling.

"What kind of counseling do you do mostly?" I inquired.

He thought for a few seconds, "Marriage counseling, probably."

"What do you tell people who have run out of affection for each other but see the value of remaining married?"

"I tell them to remember what made them fall in love in the first place. Remember why you admired each other, why you wanted to spend all day together. Remember and cultivate those affections until they outweigh what you have come to feel now."

I am sure this answer was only a small part of the difficult work that must be done to rebuild a marriage, but his injunction to remember what was good has surfaced often in my mind. As the years in ministry wear me down, I sometimes overlook what is rewarding about it and focus on what drains me, what seems unproductive, what results in conflict and misunderstanding. To those of us who have served a long time, let these pages be a call to remember what is good, what is true, and what is beautiful about life in the parsonage. To those who are just joining the ranks, may these words help you find and cherish what is good and rewarding. If you are settled into the darkest parts of ministry, allow these thoughts to be an encouragement, to nourish a hope that good can prevail.

What Is Good

In addition to my own experiences, the surveys of pastors' wives I have collected over the past thirty years have provided insight into the question "What is very rewarding, brings you the most joy, and gives you fulfillment in your role as minister's wife?" During a recent workshop at the 2009 General Assembly of the Church of the Nazarene, approximately one hundred ministry wives were surveyed. Each was asked to consider this question. The most frequent response indicated they enjoyed either ministering to or being ministered to by their congregation. Those in my national survey indicated what they like best is "being where God is at work" or "seeing God at work in the congregation" followed by both "helping people" and "working with my husband."[1]

BEING MINISTERED TO

Mary and Bob (not their real names) adopted us when we took our first church. There are very few women in the world who have as much love to give as Mary. One October night I was in the throes of premature labor pains when I called Mary. This baby was not due for another four months, and the consistent, slow progress of these intensifying contractions indicated this was not false labor. My husband and I were filled with concern after talking to my obstetrician.

"Go right to the hospital," he insisted.

The little Adirondack village hospital was a far cry from the large, metropolitan university hospital where I had delivered my firstborn. She was now eighteen months old, and as I considered the trip to that tiny village hospital, I knew Mary and Bob would help us. I called, planning to drop off my toddler at Mary's house, but Mary would have none of that. She was coming over to spend the night so that my daughter would not have her sleep disrupted.

The streets were dark and shiny with a cold drizzle as my husband and I drove into the lighted parking lot of the emergency room that midnight. Through the following hours of labor and delivery, I had no worry for my daughter; she was with Mary and Bob. A tiny boy was born that night and struggled to breathe for a brief time. Too soon he was swept into the hands of the one who said, "Let the little children come to me" (Luke 18:16). I wept, and later Mary and Bob comforted my husband and me.

Being adopted into the family of a couple we'll call Gary and Sue has been a highlight of our current ministry. They are younger, with five children, all of whom have grown into young adulthood during our ministry here. They have been sweet examples of parental love. They have been laity whom any congregation would be proud to claim. Volunteering is a way of life for them, and they have taught their children the beauty of serving others, the joy of family, and the value of people over things. They have blessed us with their thoughtful ways. Gary is the handyman who stops over to bring me mulch for my garden, fix my bathroom light, and gather the team of women and men who put a new roof on the parsonage. The whole family has been with us for more than thirty years, helping make spring flowers appear in my garden, giving of their marvelous musical talents to the church, serving in leadership positions consistently, and most of all revealing a quiet, selfless, generous faith.

There are these kind and gracious people in every church who bring so much joy to our ministry. They are very much like the loving people of Philippi whom Paul referred to in the first chapter of his letter to them when he wrote, "In all my prayers for all of you, I always pray with joy" (v. 4).

In your service at their church, remember these people, these stars of the kingdom. When you consider what ministry is, remember the grace of God that has given you these people. It is lovely; it is beautiful.

It is easier to feel the pressure from those in your congregation who struggle interminably because of poor choices. They can press on the tender nerves of your consciousness until you throb with their battles. Release these to God, but remember: fill your heart with what is good, what is true, the kind deeds rendered by the stars of the kingdom.

MINISTERING WHERE GOD IS AT WORK

Then there are those who bring great joy to us as we minister to them. One spring Sunday morning a girl we'll call Kristin first came to our church with her sister we'll call Marie. While growing up they had attended for a brief period of time a mainline Protestant church in our area. When we first met, Kristin had not had contact with any church or with the things of God for many years and came to our church this particular Sunday because of Marie's insistence. From the moment she stepped into the sanctuary, she later told us, she knew this experience was unlike any she had had before. She sat through the sermon and wept silently as God's Word and His conviction were revealed. Uncertain, she stood perplexed during the invitation extended at the end of the message then sat abjectly at the close of the benediction. Marie sat beside her as people drifted out into the sunny parking lot.

I stood at the back of the sanctuary preparing to leave as Kristin and Marie rose and began their exit. When they reached me, Kristin was weeping. I asked her if she wanted to pray about what was troubling her and she did. We prayed together, and on that joyous morning Kristin was born into the kingdom of God in the presence of Marie, God, and me.

It has been amazing to see what God has done in Kristin's life in the last twenty-something years. She is now on the pathway to ordination, has served as our associate pastor, has completed undergraduate and graduate degrees, and now is a probation officer helping young men and women turn their lives around. Her testimony is a blessing to our church. With great joy I reflect on God's grace to me through her. These changed lives—the ones we have prayed over, wept over, and rejoiced in—bring great joy to serving in the parsonage.

Paul refers to this kind of joy often in his letters to the Philippians and Thessalonians. Much of Philippians is a love letter to wonderful people Paul has had the privilege of nurturing. Serving them had been his "joy and crown" (Philippians 4:1; see 1:25-26; 2:19; 1 Thessalonians 2:19; 3:9).

Two of the great joys of being in this position are ministering to and being ministered to. Certainly lay people find similar joy in serving and being served in much the same way. But for us who find our role that of a shepherdess, the congregation can provide openness to ministry and a welcome unique to our position. Remember these who have brought you joy and celebrate them. Celebrate what God has given you in them and what He is doing in their lives because you came and stepped into their families.

WORKING WITH MY HUSBAND

A third great joy in ministry is watching God fulfill His work through your husband. When we gather into the life of a man we have chosen to love and who has received a special invitation from God to share the gospel with others, to varying degrees we live vicariously through that call. We love to join his successes, comfort him in his difficulties, and rejoice with him as he gathers his flock. A retired pastor's wife once told me that her greatest joy in her role is watching her husband stand before a congregation and come alive with energy, conviction, and eagerness to proclaim a message he has received from a faithful God.

ADOPTED FAMILY

There are some pastors' wives who want to remain quietly in the background with no more obligation or responsibility to the congregation than those of a doctor's wife to his patients or a teacher's wife to his students.

I'm not sure that choice is ours unless we insist on it. For most of us, when we step into the parsonage we step into the lives of the people. Many see us as family; we are adopted. They want us to be part of births and graduation celebrations, their dark times, their funerals, their hospital stays. They often gather us into their current events and their futures—their best and worst of times. It can be frustrating if the adopting family is dysfunctional or very needy. It can bring enormous joy if the family is loving and kingdom-focused. In every church there are sprinklings of each. Sometimes we struggle with the needy family, but often we feel entirely blessed to be part of the loving, gracious family.

Have you ever walked into a classroom or potluck dinner or party where you knew no one? Have you ever sat next to people who are so absorbed with their friends that you pass the evening without any personal contact? Have you been to a church where no one greets you or to a meeting where you are not even acknowledged? Remember those feelings? Those of us who are in ministry have the privilege of walking into any church function known by all, acknowledged by many, loved by some, respected by most. In the church where we serve, we have the incredible privilege of being known, maybe on a superficial level if we choose, but recognized and acknowledged.

REAL JOY

Consider this: While circumstances in our ministry may fuel joy, lasting joy is a gift from the Holy Spirit (1 Thessalonians 1:6). It is a fruit that develops around the seed of Christ-priority (Galatians 5:22). It is not dependent on the kindness and maturity of the congregation or our husband's successes and ministries. It is not the happiness that comes from temporal blessings, membership growth, or increases in offerings. It is the deep sense of peace that comes as we wrap our souls around God. It withstands the massive winds of circumstance, loss of members, betrayal by a close friend, or the loneliness of living in a glass house. Joy is deep, but it is not cheap.

I grew up in New Orleans, the Big Easy. My childhood was filled with the events of the small church my father pastored, with the flourishes of big city life, Mardi Gras, summer humidity, tropical fruits, and storms that brushed into the Gulf of Mexico regularly. When I was a child I remember being delighted at any radio announcement that a hurricane was coming our way. The storms we suffered then were mostly benign and resulted in street flooding, days off school, pirogue (small, Cajun, flat-bottom boats) rides down the side streets of my neighborhood, and finding tadpoles or frogs in the floodwaters near my house. I had no concept of the dangers that accompany the destructive hurricanes that blew across the southern towns at the fringes of the Gulf.

I recall hearing a description of the frenzied waters pounding the oil rigs perched along the coastal waters of Louisiana. The winds and crashing waves tore at the rigs and drove the offshore oil workers to seek shelter on shore. Those stories were filled with danger and gave me a small glimpse of the apprehension suffered by the oil workers. I have been told, however, that beneath the turbulence, down where the oil rigs are fastened to the floor of the Gulf, there is perfect quiet and stillness that defies the circulating winds of any hurricane.

Joy is like that stillness. It is the gift given by the Holy Spirit and anchors us to an eternal quiet, a gentle peace, while the waves of circumstance seethe around us, angrily shearing our happiness. So when our husbands' work seems unfruitful, when the church does not show kindness, and we struggle to see growth or maturity in the lives of our parishioners, the gift of joy as it matures can be at work in the deep roots of our souls.

In Luke 6:22-23, Jesus is enjoining the disciples to "leap for joy" when people hate them and when they are excluded and reviled and spurned because of the Son of Man. There is something deep in these waters of adversity—a gift of joy that sees the ultimate future, the rewards of heaven, our hope in Christ, the daily ministering of the Holy Spirit—and we can rejoice.

In his book *What Jesus Demands from the World*, John Piper suggests that when we find "joy" in lesser things, the opinions of others, the respect of our peers or church members, the numerical growth of our congregation, it is then that God calls us to be mastered by a deeper, ultimate joy; to count as secondary the other joys and embrace the one that cannot be disturbed by stormy circumstances.[2] "The kingdom of heaven is like treasure hidden in a field, which a man found and covered up. Then *in his joy* he goes and sells all that he has and buys that field" (Matthew 13:44, ESV, emphasis mine). He surrenders the joy of lesser things for the joy that cannot fade. It does not mean we fail to find pleasure in watching the church mature or our Sunday School classes grow; these are rewarding experiences. Jesus calls us to live in a greater joy; the joy in God, His Son, our eternal reward, and the joys given to us by the Holy Spirit. As C. S. Lewis concluded:

> If we consider the unblushing promises of reward and the staggering nature of the rewards promised in the Gospels, it would seem that our Lord finds our desires not too strong, but too weak. We are half-hearted creatures, fooling about with drink and sex and ambition when infinite joy is offered us, like an ignorant child who wants to go on making mud pies in a slum because he cannot imagine what is meant by the offer of a holiday at the sea. We are far too easily pleased.[3]

Remember the good things about ministry: the pleasures of serving or being served, of belonging. Understand the deeper joy of a faithful, caring Father.

In the next chapter you will be introduced to the number one frustration of women in ministry, what most women feel about it, and how they grow through the triumph over it.

■ FOR YOUR CONSIDERATION

1. Remember the people who have served as an example to you in the churches you have led. Thank God for them and share your thanksgiving with them. What people are you most thankful for in your present church?

2. Think of the lives you have impacted and served. Who are the people you have ministered to and rejoiced with in their growth?

3. Rejoice that God has conferred upon your husband a special calling. If you are in an active ministry now, thank God He has given him a place—a congregation to work out that service. How do you show him your support? How does he most appreciate your support?

4. Read the scriptures mentioned on previous pages that refer to the joy of the Lord. Meditate on what brings you happiness and what brings you true joy.

5. Consider John Piper's statement: "We renounce all those joy-giving things because we have found the treasure hidden in the field and we have been given eyes to see that this treasure—this glorious God—is infinitely more valuable than everything we possess or could possess in this world. This is why we renounce it all with joy."[4] What does this means to you?

FOUR

Your Expectations

A wonderful gift may not be wrapped as you expect. (Jonathan Lockwood Huie)

*W*hen the women in my survey were asked to choose the source of their greatest pressure, most of them said the pressure was self-imposed. Seventy-eight percent of the women in my survey experienced occasional discouragement, dysthymia, or depression caused by their own perfectionism, low self-esteem, unrealistic goals, negativity, or feelings of failure; essentially unrealistic expectations about themselves.

As I began this book, the task of writing this chapter loomed large, because this topic is one that most of us struggle with. We are encouraged to reach high and plan big, but we often get lost in distinguishing between these external goals and our internal self-worth. It becomes increasingly difficult to separate our self-esteem from our aspirations. When aspirations are not realized, self-esteem suffers. *I am what I dream, so if my dreams fail, I am a failure.*

Then there are the unrealistic expectations we bring to the congregations in our churches. How do we manage these and bring them into an appropriate perspective?

Self-Expectations

"I feel that I am supposed to be perfect spiritually, physically, psychologically. Somewhere in the past, I drew a picture of the role of a ministry wife, and now I struggle to live up to that image. I stretch to do jobs too tall for me, that don't come anywhere near my giftedness, and after any failure I am defeated. I am so busy doing too many things that none of them gets done well."

The Christian education director asks a new ministry wife to lead Vacation Bible School. Her thoughts begin, *If I try, this will be the worst VBS ever. I have no skills to lead. I am so unqualified, but someone has to do it. I can see disaster coming, but I am the pastor's wife, and I should be able to take a leadership role.*

These are classic cases of "unrelenting standards," and that is the number one source of pressure experienced by ministry wives questioned in my survey. Not pressure from other people, the church, from husband or family, but from oneself. *I am supposed to be able to do this impossible thing, but I am so not able to do it,* is the emerging message coursing through the mind, the inner critic's voice that all too often predicts certain failure. The result can be a feeling of great discouragement with all the felt demands of ministry.

The official definition of this self-critical mind-set called unrelenting standards is given by Jeffrey Young, assistant clinical professor of psychology, UCLA:

> The underlying belief that one must strive to meet very high internalized standards of behavior and performance, usually to avoid criticism. Typically results in feelings of pressure or difficulty slowing down; and in hypercriticalness toward oneself and others. [The clinical diagnosis]

must involve significant impairment in: pleasure, relaxation, health, self-esteem, sense of accomplishment, or satisfying relationships.

Unrelenting standards typically present as: (a) perfectionism, inordinate attention to detail, or an underestimate of how good one's own performance is relative to the norm; (b) rigid rules and "shoulds" in many areas of life, including unrealistically high moral, ethical, cultural, or religious precepts; or (c) preoccupation with time and efficiency, so that more can be accomplished.[1]

Unrelenting standards, seen as insistent self-criticism, often forge one rail of the tracks upon which depression and anxiety progress. David M. Dunkley of McGill University, Canada, suggested in a recent study that the most self-critical were also the most likely to be depressed and have difficulties with interpersonal relationships years later.[2]

Some years ago, I was diagnosed with cancer. If you have received such a diagnosis you will understand the strangling fear that surrounds it. My quiet nights were often interrupted by a gripping fright of the future, an agonizing feeling that all I knew and loved would disappear in pain and unimaginable decline, and that my family would suffer because of my untimely death. During that time I heard again and again from healthcare professionals that my thought patterns and gut responses would actually affect the outcome of my disease; that the adrenalin/cortisone releasing bursts of fear would diminish my immune system's ability to fight off the cancer. After much grace from God, my mantra became, "I will not worry about this—or anything—because the worry itself can contribute to the decline I fear." I viewed it as though releasing the fear was a health tonic, a prescription for healthy living, an invisible pill that would restore my physical equilibrium.

In the same way, discovering that your persistent self-critic may damage the outcome of the situation you are addressing may help you realize the need to change your pattern of thinking. People respond to you the way you think they will. The way you see yourself and your limitations can be challenged and can evolve into something positive and useful.

Unrelenting standards often spring from perfectionism—an insidious thief of joy. Our daily mental intake too often claims that if we are not perfect, shame on us. There is a treatment, a diet, a pill, that will bring us to the perfection displayed in the glossy pictures of women's magazines or the sparkling ads reaching out from television commercials. We are led to believe that perfection is within our reach if we buy, believe, or embrace what is proffered. Sometimes this quest for perfection, nurtured in the secular, sloshes over into the spiritual. Our service to God can and must be perfect if only we pray more, meditate on God's Word, or discipline ourselves enough. We believe we can serve God perfectly. This approach can lead to dishonesty in order to keep up appearances, illusions that we have to be in control, denial that we are imperfect, defensiveness, and most of all great spiritual exhaustion.

Anne Wilson Schaef describes this perfectionism as an addiction in her book *When Society Becomes an Addict:*

> It may be hard to picture addicts as conscientious, concerned people with high aspirations and high expectations of themselves, but that is what most of them are. Alcoholics, drug addicts, and compulsive overeaters are perfectionists. They are convinced that nothing they do is ever good

enough, that they don't do as much as they should, and that they can be perfect if only they figure out how.

Those who treat addicts consider perfectionism to be a major stumbling block to recovery. . . . It is difficult to help addicts forgive themselves for not being perfect and perceive themselves as good people anyway. They persist in viewing themselves as *bad* people trying to become good, not sick people trying to get well.[3]

Managing the Unrelenting Standards

Climbing out of this trap of unrelenting standards begins with "I can do everything through him who gives me strength" (Philippians 4:13). This verse is not a command to do everything; it is a confirmation that Christ will walk with you as you do what He has called you to do. If you can get your heart around the sense of this verse, then with Christ-confidence take some steps toward the goal of release, you will be given the grace. Sometimes, tiny bits of grace are sprinkled on your pathway because your feet can only move a tiny bit, but each bit moves you to a tiny success, then to a growing belief in what God can do in you.

Katherine Muller, director of psychology training at Montefiore Medical Center in Bronx, New York, gives several practical suggestions for second steps in this process. She is quoted in the article by Melinda Beck of the *Wall Street Journal*.[4] Muller's suggestions are combined with those gleaned from my survey of ministry wives and are given for your consideration.

Monitor your thoughts. This is something like recording calories when you are dieting. There is something so enlightening and foundational about stopping to recognize and bring to surface level your subconscious mental gatherings. What are you feeding on mentally? Are you dwelling on the outward successes of others? Does the memory of that perfect pastor's wife course like a riptide under the surface of your self-evaluations? Keep a notebook or write in your personal electronic device every critical self-judgment, every perfectionist idea you have about yourself. Do it for a week. Keep track of the circumstances that provoked these thoughts. You may see a pattern emerge. For me the self-doubts come whenever someone I have cared for or prayed over leaves our church. Every time this happens, I find myself saying "If only I could have been better at . . . ," essentially blaming myself for the painful loss. Stop and recognize the self-blame for what it is.

Evaluate your judgments. Examine your standards to see if they are realistic, fair, or reasonable. Do you blame yourself for a decline in church attendance or the small turnout for the children's day program? Depersonalize what you cannot change. If an agitated family decides to leave the church, quit asking yourself what is wrong with you and realistically look at what is beyond your control to change. "They left because they are uncomfortable with the expression of emotional joy in our church. That is who we are and who we should be. It is what it is, let it be." Or "Their teens did not engage with our teen program, for whatever reason. This is not my failure."

You may have some role to play in the failure. Evaluate realistically what it may be. It is sometimes difficult, but make a distinction between thinking intently on a situation or occasion and worrying about it. Thinking intently is productive, worry is not. Worry increases blood pressure, disquiet, and fear. Thinking intently can direct your mind to possible causes and solutions. It is impersonal and more logical. You can look at the attitudes in your life that should be adjusted, gather an understanding of what can be helpful, and galvanize a plan of action. "Is there a general reason the music team seems to lack unity? Could it be they need more prayer time together or need to be more supportive of each other?" rather than "I should be more involved in the music team. If I had more time to have them over for dinner, this situation might be better. But I am so overwhelmed. I can't do this ministry wife thing. It is too difficult. I am incompetent." Recognize this is a downward spiral.

Evaluate whether or not you are liable. Consider your liabilities objectively. Does the responsibility lie with someone else? If so, pray for that person and give up the self-condemnation. Let the surfacing of these thoughts trigger a silent prayer for the one who is responsible. Cut yourself off from the condemnation. Joyce Meyer says, "The most foolish thing in the world is to try to do something about something you cannot do anything about."[5]

This is a lot easier said than done. But, like most of life's progress, it takes practice and grace.

Collect objective data then celebrate your progress. In my survey women were divided into four groups based on their response to a detailed descriptive question about their experience with discouragement, dysthymia, or depression. The first of the four groups reported that they very rarely became discouraged about ministry. The second group reported they occasionally felt discouraged about ministry. The third and fourth groups reported having experienced dysthymia (a more protracted but milder form of depression) or depression during their time in ministry.

When asked, "What helps you most during this period of discouragement, dysthymia, or depression?" the number two answer related to a positive attitude. Fifty-five percent of the first group indicated they would advise women in ministry to maintain some form of positive thinking, mental optimism.

Here's how positive thinking or optimism can play out. Mentally collect and celebrate the things you do well. Celebration and enjoyment are an indispensable part of life. They bring emotional and spiritual health. The Old Testament is full of feasts and celebrations; the Feast of Unleavened Bread, of First Fruits, the Passover, to name a few. These are celebrations of God's work. Every day can be a celebration of what God has done in your life. Be excited about your progress regardless of how small it seems. Instead of collecting the failures of the day, collect and celebrate the progress of the day. Make small note cards of your accomplishments to review when the tyrant of self-criticism emerges. Make and collect note cards that include scripture verses that let you know who you are in Christ, what hope you can have in His continued work in your life. Give yourself a break, God is not finished with you yet.

Being confident of this, that he who began a good work in you will carry it on to completion until the day of Christ Jesus. (Philippians 1:6)

This celebration spirit may take discipline—more for some women than for others—and will take grace, but practicing this discipline will bring healing. God has given us a spirit of discipline and self-control according to 2 Timothy 1:7. It is one of the fruit of the Spirit. It looks something like this:

I will praise you, God, for the control you gave me to remain silent when I wanted to strike out against that busybody. Thank you, God, for the grace victory of a quiet tongue,

rather than

I am so upset! I wish I had given her a piece of my mind, but I know that's not what God wants. I feel guilty that it's so hard to love that woman. I can't seem to get this thing right.

This does not mean that you deny having thoughts of raking her over the coals. But notice that in the first example the focus is on thankfulness, God's victory in your life, not you and your response.

If we can celebrate and mark with joy the progress of the past or even of the day, we will be less often consumed by worry over what will transpire in the future. It is a discipline, and discipline can be a large contributor to freedom. It is work, but it beats living an out-of-control life smeared with spiritual exhaustion.

This will take prayer. In my survey, the number one response to the completion statement "I deal with the pressures of ministry by . . ." was prayer. In a follow-up question, the number one answer given about what helped when dark times came and the number one piece of advice from those who were rarely discouraged was some form of spiritual discipline—personal devotions, prayer, Bible study, or meditation. I'm thinking this is not the wringing-your-hands-before-God kind of prayer, but a rejoicing, thankful repetition of what God has done in your life, the victories of personal growth, the sometimes tiny bits of progress He has blessed you with today, a petition to see God do it again in the situation you now face. In Philippians 4:6 we are told to be anxious about nothing, but in everything we are to pray and be thankful.

Joyce Meyer calls the celebration of yourself a come-as-you-are party.[6] There is no need to feel that you have to change clothes or habits before you join God's celebration of you. Come celebrate what God has already done. And if you look carefully, you will see what changes He has already made in your life. You may feel that the changes have not come yet or are coming too slowly. Look a little harder, work on your spirit of hope. Ask God to help you celebrate. *I am not incompetent. I can love this unlovable woman. I can trust you, God, for my finances. I can do this thing through Christ. I will hold myself tall and smile in the hope of what God is going to do. If it does not turn out the way I hope, then I will rejoice in the new lesson that you will teach me.*

Distinguish between constructive correction and fruitless guilt. Is this guilt or godly correction? The goal of each uncomfortable encounter should be improvement. Both guilt and godly correction can be uncomfortable. Discern in the latter what the lesson is for you, glean it, and then move on. Refuse to let fruitless guilt batter you. Instead of thinking *I am a terrible person because I did not speak out for my faith in that school board meeting,* think *I will think about and practice what I can say next time and be ready.* Then pray that God will give you courage and will open the door for you.

Condemnation is painful but unproductive. Corrective thinking is sometimes painful, but if we are intent upon the lessons it gives, it can be a time of enrichment. There are different seasons of life, some for great joy, some for great and painful growth, some for self-denial, some for extended celebration. "There is a time for everything, and a season for every activity under heaven" (Ecclesiastes 3:1). The correction season is not often a season of comfort or great joy, but it can be endured with stability and balance. The first few years of ministry may be a time of correction—of false assumptions, of unreasonable expectations. However, evaluating each distressing event to de-

Therefore, there is now no
in Christ Jesus. (Romans 8.

Check what you value. B
able about is worth it. Some goa
ful in the eyes of your peers or
a fashion journal, are not worth
moil. Other goals, like pleasing
possess. Don't allow unworthy g

Love yourself as God love
says you are His works and His
wonderfully made; but more tha
wonderful. Think about that for
heart and mind and gather up the
Then the light of God can reflec
its bright colors and unique patte
precious daughter. When His love
catch a glimpse of this daughter o
value He places on you and wants

At the end of a summer day
and sisters and I drove to what w
an adjacent city in south Louisian
white clapboard church where pe
our denomination gathered to hea
can country.

I settled into the front seat, a
ing, I watched as the large-framed
platform. The soft hum of electric f
My feet swung back and forth in ne
to the pulpit. I don't remember all
told, but to this day I can remembe
it. Now, even more, after having sp

termine what is the correction to keep and what is the condemnation to discard is of great value.

Joyce Meyer endured a season of self-denial when God was at work teaching her valuable lessons. I suspect from the context of her story that this was a time of financial tension. "We all have times like this and it is important to be able to flow in and out of the various seasons of our lives comfortably. If I have to shop for earrings or Dave [her husband] has to go to the golf store to be happy, then we have a problem, but if it is something we simply enjoy, then God will sanction it and even help us find what we are looking for."[7] Equanimity in turmoil, flowing in and out of discomfort with grace and peace, sounds like an oxymoron, but it can happen. Learning it is what is called *practiced habituation.*

Habituation can be a good thing or a bad thing. I teach elementary education majors a course in biology that prepares them to understand the basics of the living environment. One of the chapters I cover is on animal behavior, and one of the animal behaviors we discuss is habituation. It's the behavior that is expressed as a seagull chick learns to distinguish between the shadow of a dangerous predator flying above and the shadow of a falling leaf.

Shortly after the chick is born it cowers from every moving shadow overhead. Over time and with experience, the chick cowers only upon the appearance of a predator rather than the sighting of a drifting leaf. That's habituation. Notice it takes time.

The first time we are confronted with an overwhelming challenge in ministry—a request to take charge of the Sunday School program or the realization that we cannot accomplish all that we have agreed to do—we may cower, ready to pack up and run. We may be hyper‹

self-blame. *I am frightened to*

can't do what is expected of ‹

pastor's wife I knew when I ‹

everything right.

With practice we learn to d

terns that are destructive an‹

tween what is predatory self-‹

the shadow of a leaf—a helpful

ships. With practice we learn h‹

to pull hard on God's grace, t‹

realize what is within our gifte

all we learn to say no when we

and without guilt. "We really d‹

musician for VBS. I genuinely ‹

but let's put our heads together

with for some other kind of mus‹

Give up the guilt about wh‹

and drives you away from God.

to hide from Him, like Adam di‹

when I had trouble even listenii

it made me feel guilty. It wasn't t

song but the concept that God v

reminder of Him made me uncoi

condemnation. I was not good ei

distance. Not estranged, but dist

other hand, will help us see the

can take to make progress. Joyce

for guilt. That's how *no condemn*

of the accuser, not God. Give you‹

on the guilt.

Kenya, Africa, where the practice of bride price is still held in high regard, I value this story.

In an upcountry African village there lived a young man who was longing for a wife of great value. In the culture of his homeland, it was the custom to offer a bride price to the family of the bride as part of the engagement process. A bride price of two or three cows was an offer made for an average woman, and a bride price of five cows was one made for a woman of great beauty, education, and cultural value. This young man searched among the women of his village and settled on one he particularly admired. For her he offered ten cows.

The story of this ten cow bride spread around the area and into the neighboring villages until it was finally relayed to the missionary who lived quite some distance from the couple. He was curious enough to visit the quiet village one sweltering summer afternoon in order to see the great beauty of this bride. The sun was intense upon the copper colored mud of the road into the village. When he came into the village center he inquired about the young man and his new bride. He was directed to a small, dusty, brown hut near the edge of the village, and it was there he went to have a look for himself. As he walked up to the home of the couple he noticed a very plain young woman working in the garden, collecting the maize and vegetables for the day. He greeted her and spoke a few words of common courtesy, then turned in the direction of the hut.

He called out, hoping to arouse the man of the house, and soon the husband appeared in the doorway. They greeted one another and the missionary was invited in to enjoy a cup of bush tea with the husband. After a time of conversation and discussion of the topics of the day, the missionary asked the husband, "Where is your wife?"

"Oh, she is out collecting vegetables in the garden," he replied. "Shall I call her in?"

The missionary was puzzled. Could the very plain, quiet young woman be the bride of ten cows? Because he had traveled a long distance, and because he was very curious, he dared to ask a personal question.

"The woman in the garden, is she your wife?"

"Yes, she is my bride."

"She appears to be a kind and good wife, but may I ask why you paid ten cows for her?"

The young man's reply surprised even the seasoned missionary.

"I want her to always remember how valuable she is to me. To me she is a ten cow bride."

To God, we are a bride beyond price. It matters less how we are valued by others. He has given His best for us, not ten cows or a thousand cows, but His own Son, because we are of such great value to Him. Love yourself as God loves and values you beyond price.

Give up the comparisons. In 2 Corinthians 10:12, Paul indicates the folly of comparing ourselves with each other. "For we are not bold to class or compare ourselves with some of those who commend themselves; but when they measure themselves by themselves and compare themselves with themselves, they are without understanding." It appears from this verse that we are foolish when we compare our lives to others' lives and long to be like someone else.

When you find yourself practicing this comparison game, or you find yourself filled with self-criticism about what you are not, give it up. Remember to monitor your thoughts, evaluate your judgments, collect objective data, and celebrate your progress. Distinguish between constructive correction and fruitless guilt. Love yourself as God loves you.

God is not demanding perfection. He is encouraging risk and growth. He is not demanding that I be nice; He wants me to live in truth. He is not demanding I stay young; He wants me to live in reality. He is not demanding that I be sophisticated; He wants me to live simply with Him.

He asks me to let go of unrealistic expectations of my world and myself—these unrealistic expectations that steal my joy—the joy of being me. If I let go of what *they* say, maybe I can listen to more of what He is saying.[8]

Expectations You Have for Ministry

"One out of ten ministers will actually retire as a minister in some form."[9] Too many ministers leave before they have found the stable rhythm of the ministry. The reasons are diverse and complex, but one of the main explanations is, arguably, disillusionment. It's just not what we thought it would be. The expectations often begin in seminary when descriptions of the ministry enthrall us. Having few reality checks from people in ministry—or more likely being unable to hear the reality checks—the picture gets rosier each chapel service or each seminar. We are young and idealistic. This is reflected in the research of Robert Ayling in his study of student ministers' wives. He surveyed the wives of seminary students at Boston University School of Theology, Southern Baptist Seminary, Garrett Theological Institute, and Yale Divinity School:

> The seminary wives expect themselves to act differently as a minister's wife than if they were not. They expect

themselves to be examples, to participate more actively in church and community affairs, and to be more ideal in personality or more congenial in disposition. In the same way, they believe that their husbands and their husbands' congregations will have expectations of them that they would not have if their husbands were in another vocation. They believe these expectations to be identical to those expectations they have of themselves. In addition, they feel that their husbands expect them to understand and share their vocations and the demands that vocation makes.[10]

The idealism continues when the church interviews the prospective pastor. Everyone is working hard to give a good impression, and rightfully so. A first impression is a lasting one. Unfortunately, most of us bring to this situation all the expectations and hopes we can muster. The church hires its sterling new minister; in his mind he sees a vision of what the church will look like in ten years, what the people will cooperate to accomplish, then the honeymoon period bursts out of the starting block. Within the first few years, the hopes we built around what would take place often begin to evaporate, the ideal pastor-leader image begins to tarnish in the presence of the pressure of reality.

The congregation says he does not preach as well as they thought he would, and he doesn't visit people as they had hoped. The pastor thinks the financial support is not what was implied when he interviewed for the position, and there are no leaders in the church who will embrace his vision for the church. "They say they want to grow, but they are not taking any of the steps necessary for that to happen! It's just not what I expected." And on it goes.

The pastor moves on to a new church, hoping to find the "right fit." He leaves behind some broken relationships and some key people who leave the church. The ministry wife feels angry about the way he was treated and silently soldiers on. Disillusionment increases every time greater value is placed on the things that are not happening and the people who are obstructionists rather than the gracious people or the good things that God is bringing about in the church. Some things take time, and everything takes grace and love.

Inflated expectations are especially found in the church because we are blessed with the power of the Holy Spirit that gives an added boost to the belief that all things can and will be accomplished because God is in them.

Managing Expectations of the Ministry

The first few months in a new setting are often referred to as the honeymoon period, which means expectations are high and have yet to meet reality. When reality dawns it sometimes brings disappointment or frustration; then the real work of grace, flexibility, and compromise begins. Ways to diminish the strain of this work were suggested by women experienced in the skill of ministry living.

Understand, ferret out the expectation. The business world is full of advice on how to manage the expectations of clients. At the top of most how-to lists is clearly identifying expectations.

List the expectations. Bring them to the front of your consciousness. Write them down. Most of us believe we will be appreciated for our sacrifices, that people will love us for our good deeds, and that the church will flourish and increase numerically if we do our best in the jobs we undertake. This is probably true most of the time, but when it is not, the expectation should be recognized. Whatever your expectations are, identify them so they may be examined.

Determine the root of your expectations. Childhood memories may impact your view of what is to be expected at a church. As children and young people, we are often sheltered from the more negative side of church interactions. Relying on past memories of a conflict-free church to set the standards for the current church is unrealistic. Recognize that many of these expectations are based on immature perceptions.

Even naive perceptions we construct as adults can be misleading. No matter how ideal a neighboring church may appear, we are not in possession of all the facts. If the root of our expectations lives in the picture of that ideal church, we need to examine that root.

Give your expectations to God rather than placing them on the shoulders of others. Take the expectation list you made and place it firmly in His hands.

There is a sequence of requests and an interesting consequence Jesus sets out:

But love your enemies, do good to them, and lend to them *without expecting to get anything back*. Then your reward will be great, and you will be sons of the Most High, because he is kind to the ungrateful and wicked. (Luke 6:35, emphasis added)

You will save yourself much frustration if you can give without expecting to be rewarded by the church for your giving.

Notice, however, there are great rewards, just not always from the church you serve. It is easy to expect that if we attend every baby shower, wedding shower, funeral, and graduation party, and if we work hard at the tasks of churchmanship, people will respond positively, appreciate us, and regularly express their appreciation. Better you should hand off to God all your good deeds as flowers and build a bouquet of exquisite beauty for Him. Lay them in His hands and know beyond doubt that He appreciates and rejoices in them and the rewards that really matter will be great. Look past the recipients of the shower gifts and place the deed into the hands of Jesus. Free the receiving family from your expectations for thank-you notes and approval. God has promised He will reward you richly.

When the church does not seem to appreciate your husband or the effort, and love you have expended upon a family does not bear fruit, if you have given all these things as a gift to God, He will issue the rewards in His time.

Don't be guilty of silent gratitude. The very appreciation that encourages you will bless others as you practice it. Express gratitude to people who show kindness or do a job well. You might even start a thankfulness trend. Be the example.

What Can You Expect?

What do other ministry wives say you might expect from the ministry? This often depends on the church situation, your health, your age, your experience, and other factors. But in general most ministry wives are positive, fulfilled, challenged, would like to see some things changed, and enjoy what they are doing most of the time. Keep in mind that for seventy-three percent of us there are times of real discouragement, and for some, frustrating, debilitating darkness. It is for those times and for those seventy-three percent this book is written. But always, always keep perspective on this. For most of us the times of discouragement are, in the great scheme of things, transient. Life goes on, and the grace of God works to draw us into His Sonlight for times of joy and fulfillment.

Even with all the statistics out there, it is safe to say that your experience will be unique. You bring to the church your unique set of gifts and challenges. The church brings to you a very different set of strengths and challenges. Most of us have found that in spite of the diverse gifts and challenges, life as a ministry wife is good. Expect good most of the time, understand the bad will come occasionally, and stay close to God to guide you when you encounter bumps in the road.

What about expectations that other people have for you or criticisms that spring from other people's unmet expectations? Is there anything that can be done to help overcome these? Let's look at that in the next chapter.

■ FOR YOUR CONSIDERATION

1. How well do you think you fulfill the responsibilities of being a ministry wife on a scale of 1 to 10, with 10 being very well? Explain.
2. What characteristic about yourself is most helpful in your church tasks?
3. What would you change about yourself if you could?
4. Do you see any connection between these two? In other words, do your weaknesses arise from some aspect of your strengths?
5. How can you minimize your weaknesses without feeling guilty they exist?
6. How can you celebrate your strengths?

FIVE

Expectations of Others

Am I prisoner of people's expectations or liberated by Divine promises? (Henri Nouwen)

*H*er husband was presenting himself as a candidate to be the church's new pastor. She sat with him in a small Sunday School classroom and studied the faces of the nine women and men on the church board who were to decide their future. They were kindly faces, full of a mixture of hope, concern, and uncertainty. When they had exhausted most of the questions directed at her husband, they turned to her with expectant faces.

"Would you teach a Sunday School class for the teens and consider directing a choir?" That was the beginning. Something about her personality, about the request, about the pressure of the moment sent a line of tension in her heart. The mound of presumptions felt like a tower of great expectations. She felt like a marching band under review by the judges who would determine her ranking among all the others. Feeling at a disadvantage because of her young age, she felt answerable to this group of well-meaning but overly expectant board members. She gave no hint of her resentment, but these thoughts remained unexpressed, unreleased.

She was six months pregnant, so she suggested she should probably wait a bit before determining just where she would serve in the church. Good answer. She was not aware of the full force of the continuing standards of behavior, dress, and performance others would impose on her. In the years ahead she would face debilitating exhaustion, because she did not recognize the power the approval of others generated.

The eventual burnout that accompanies what Joyce Meyer calls "approval addiction" is described clearly below:

Often ministry wives so desperately want to please that they do everything they feel is expected of them and then some. They may be committed to being "nice." Sometimes they say yes just because they cannot say no, not because they think their actions are the will of God. They burn out for lack of discernment or because of unwarranted guilt. And so, also, their anger builds.

We become angry when we feel all used up and pulled in every direction. . . . We become angry with the people pressuring us, when in reality we are allowing ourselves to be pressured. To avoid pressure from others and from ourselves, we must take control of our lives under the guidance of the Holy Spirit.[1]

It seems there is a confluence of events and conditions that bring us closer to burnout in our thirties than at any other time in our lives. That is when I went through my darkest moments. If you are in these early years of ministry and struggling to live up to the unrealistic expectations of others, recognize this is a vulnerable time in your life. Ask people you love to pray that you may withstand the evil one. There is a spiritual battle emerging that requires spiritual weapons. The weapons of the enemy are guilt, condemnation, overcommitment, addiction to people's approval, disillusionment caused by unrealistic expectations, and sometimes health and finance issues. God loves you and holds out His arms to hold you and keep you from going under. Get to know the feeling of His arms around you as you pray. His voice will speak to you in His written Word. Still, no matter how you feel, He is there.

What Causes Us to Feel Encumbered by the Expectations of Others?

The expectations we place on others. We find no inconsistencies in expecting the church members to perform to a certain standard. We say, "The congregants should be aware of how they leave the church facilities on Sunday, and they should pick up after themselves. We could save a lot of money on cleaning if everyone understood this." "If everyone wants a Vacation Bible School, why do we have so much trouble getting teachers for it? Every church mother who has children that come to VBS should be willing to work with a class of girls and boys, or at least sit with them in crafts or during recreation."

The more resolute we are in our expectations of others, the more we feel the pressure from them to conform to their expectations. It's such an irony.

The congregation's pleasant memories of the past. External expectations also come from something H. B. London and Neil Wiseman call "group memories."[2] "Mrs. Hamilton used to have the church families over for dinner often. I haven't been in the parsonage in the ten years since our current pastor has been here." These kinds of statements can leave you bristling, discouraged, or puzzled. You could view them as a mandate to open hospitality or as a pleasant memory of an effective ministry, maybe a sentimental recollection that probably drifts slowly from reality as the years advance, or a kind statement about a woman with the gift of hospitality. The person expressing such thoughts may be expressing her disappointment in you, but she may not. She may be merely articulating a practice that is now absent. Something like we might say, "I remember when my mother used to make homemade rolls for Sunday dinner." There is no expectation in the statement, just a bit of sentimental nostalgia.

Good response: "Those are wonderful memories. Mrs. Hamilton was a woman of great hospitality. It is kind of you to remember those occasions so positively." This response puts the ball right into her court and off yours. No defensiveness here.

False assumptions. To be honest, everyone faces some unrealistic expectations based on false assumptions. They are the common source of conflict between boss and employee— "I assumed you would return my call even if I did not ask you to"—between husband and wife, between attorney and client, between parent and child.

What adds to the burden shouldered by the ministry wife is the thought that God may be involved in these expectations. He may be the one behind the assumptions of the church board or the women in the church. The bewildering array of emotions accompanying a young, free-floating faith may lend credibility to the idea that God is expecting her to be the ultimate example of Christlikeness to her church and to herself. There is no room for failure, for if she fails, the damage is irreparable.

What's the lie or false assumption here? Assuming that God shines mainly through success. The truth is that it is in the stumbling and weakness of our lives that God reveals himself as loving and merciful. It is in the failures and recoveries that grace shines out to a people clueless about grace (2 Corinthians 12:9).

The congregation's needs. "Please, consider starting a children's choir." This may be simply a call for help, a wish, a dream, not a demand.[3]

A good response would be, "Thank you for considering me, but my gifts are not with music or children. However, I will help you pray for someone who feels the burden for this ministry. Maybe we could make a list of people who might be available and gifted in this area, and we could begin by getting a committee together to review children's music that might be appropriate for our children." The best response is, "Yes, I am interested and can help you, but not in the way you perceive."

Outspoken complainers. "Bless your heart, sweetie, you probably didn't realize that sweater is not your color." And the real kicker, "And I am not the only one who thinks this way." Unfortunately, you will be stuck with a few of these in every congregation. These women and men should be loved and not taken seriously. Don't internalize their criticisms.

A good response would be, "What's your favorite color? I'll bet you look smashing in green." No internalizing here. The ball is back in her court. She is probably more interested in expressing her thoughts anyway.

Handling Unrealistic Expectations of Others

When ministry wives were asked how they manage unrealistic expectations, the most common answer was through their spiritual development (hearing God) and maturity (practicing what He says to do). What exactly does that look like in ministry?

The best way to handle the myriad of internal and external demands is not to flippantly reject them offhand or to spend your emotional currency resisting them or to resign yourself to frustrating attempts to live up to them. Rather, it is to know God's view of you and to understand your strengths and gifts and how these two—God's view and your gifts—merge into a beautiful tapestry; entirely possible and wondrously fulfilling (2 Corinthians 5:9).

Consider the following suggestions. You will find that what appear to be two seemingly different issues have been blended in these suggestions: expectations of others and criticism leveled by others. Expressed, inappropriate expectations of others can often feel like criticism. They spring from the same well. "You are too extravagant with church money" is both a criticism and an expectation that you should be spending only a certain amount of money.

Wrap Your Heart Around God's View of You

- You are God's workmanship (Ephesians 2:10).
- You are a minister of reconciliation for God (1 Corinthians 6:17-21).
- You are a branch of Jesus Christ (John 15:5a).
- You are chosen and appointed to bear fruit (John 15:5b).
- You are God's temple (1 Corinthians 3:16).
- You are a citizen of heaven (Philippians 3:20).
- You are a disciple, a friend of Jesus Christ (John 15:15).
- You have been bought with a price and belong to God (1 Corinthians 6:19-20).
- You are complete in Christ (Colossians 2:9-10).
- The work He began in you, He will complete (Philippians 1:6).

It's amazing to be God's child.

Joyce Meyer uses an illustration taken from an unidentified speaker to demonstrate our value to God:

Before he began his seminar, the speaker held up a $50 bill and asked the audience, "Who wants this $50 bill?" Brainless question, right? Everyone in the room held up a hand in response.

"What if I do this to the bill?" He continues as he wadded the bill into a tiny ball. "How many still want the bill?"

All hands rose again.

"What if I do this?" He drops the crumpled bill onto the floor of the platform and crushes it with the heel of his shoe. "How many still want the bill?"

Still all the hands rose.

The bill still held its value to each person in the room, despite its dilapidated condition. Sometimes we come to God with wrong attitudes, angry with Him, discouraged beyond faith, tired of doing good. Guess what? To Him we still hold our value. We are beyond price to Him. He won't sentence us to a closet or to a dark region for incompetents. He still thinks we are of inestimable value.[4]

Know yourself. The second half of the ticket to handling the unrealistic expectations of others is to know yourself. Learn to be confident in what you can do and comfortable with what you cannot do. Discern your spiritual gifts. Learn your boundaries. Work on the things God tells you you need help with rather than the things others say need to change. These two may often—but not always—coincide, so train yourself to distinguish between what God will give you grace to perfect and what someone else feels you need to change. When these differ, cherish the first, toss the second. Learn to trust yourself, your strengths, your intelligence, and your perspective as you mature spiritually. Know who you are in Christ.

Teresa Flint-Borden co-owned and served as a consultant in a paramedical day spa before her days as a ministry wife. She offered consultation services that included assessing the client's facial shape, hair type, body type, coloring, lifestyle; then together with physicians, dentists, psychologists, clothing designers, and others she advised women on their best choices for personal appearance and lifestyle. It was not long after she began this service that she noticed the great majority of her clients came in wanting to look like someone else—some Hollywood starlet or fashion figure. Her response was, "You need to be the very best you, as everyone else is already taken."[5]

Remember who thought you up, created you, and made you entirely special. This God, seen in Christ, has committed all His eternal resources to transforming our character into His image, to be the best you that you can be. Get to know the transforming God and His faithfulness to show you who you can be. What you will become is not Mrs. Pearson, whom you adored as your first pastor's wife, it is not the wife of the denominational leader who looks like she has it all together, or the wife of the pastor you know who seems to live in perfect peace and has answers to every perplexing question. It is the precious, special, wonderful best *you* you can be. The more we form a bond with God, the more we depend on our inner guide.

For most of us, the knowing oneself process begins with the "renewing of your mind" (Romans 12:2), because we have often bought into erroneous ideas about ourselves.

This renewing is, in my experience, a lifelong process. It is at times painful as we learn to distinguish between what God wants to do in us and what others think God wants to do in us.

With every act of God's transforming work there is a grace to endure, a thankful relief in the lessons learned, and strength beyond ourselves. It is the change in our thought patterns, our minds, and our heads that begins the transformation of our hearts. Some of us grow with a steep learning curve. Sometimes the more pain, the more gain.

To some extent, who we are is wrapped up in what we do or in what the church is doing. When we have had a plateau year or a year of decline in the church, we feel less valuable or embarrassed. The 1990 Crow survey shows that ministry wives in churches of less than one hundred use words such as "depressing" to describe their position significantly more often than those in churches of more than one hundred. It is not helpful to attach your self-image to the statistics of the church.[6]

Learning to know yourself can sometimes turn up character flaws that contribute to your frustrations about expectations. For example, you may discover that you are a people pleaser. You may have such an unhealthy need for the approval of others that you cannot be happy knowing someone objects to you or your ideas or that someone is critical of your work.

Please God first. The first step in having joy with or without the approval of others is learning that we are ultimately responsible only to pleasing God. That's a tough one if you feel that God is harsh, overbearing, and gruff, or you have based your impression of Him on authority personalities who are less than godly.

One humid spring day when I was in high school, I hurried into the kitchen of our parsonage home in the upper ninth ward of New Orleans to show my father my report card. I had worked hard and was proud that I had accomplished a high average in my class grades. I thrust my report card into his hands, and he peered through his trifocals at the comments and grades. "I see you got a ninety-six in physical education. Why didn't you get a hundred?" I was at first puzzled, then annoyed. To him, it just wasn't right; it wasn't perfect.

Somehow, I transferred that spirit of perfectionist judgment to God. If I wasn't perfect, I wasn't good enough.

God is not like that. Here are two very important ways to please Him:

1. Hebrews 11:6: He is pleased by your faith and He rewards you if you search for Him.

2. John 6:28-29: He is pleased by your belief in Jesus, His Son. This is the "work" that God requires.

There are many things we do in response to God's love, because of the overflow of His love in our lives, because of the Spirit at work in us, but these are not the things we must do to please Him.

Joyce Meyer says we are called "believers" not "achievers" for a reason.[7] Our work is to believe in Jesus Christ, to trust God's truths more than we trust the god of our feelings. There is no pressure to perform in order to please Him, nor do we have any fear of failure if our works aren't perfect.

There's a chunk of freedom here, folks. God does not reject us if what we do is done imperfectly. If we are afraid that He will reject us, that lie becomes truth to us, and we relinquish the rest He wants us to have in Him. We fret when we decline to teach a class of children in VBS or lead a women's Bible study as though we have failed God. If you have accepted that lie, you need to have your mind renewed. To think differently is to act differently. To act differently is to be different. It starts with the renewing of your mind and practiced habituation!

We want to please God by our actions, but God is interested in what is in our hearts. As long as He has our hearts, He will work on our attitudes and passions and help us with our actions. We may be sour or have a critical spirit or hold grudges, but as long as He has our intentions, He who began a good work in us will finish it and work on the attitude.

Now in my forty-second year of ministry, I can assure you He has been at work on my heart, my attitudes, and my actions all these years, and I am much farther along the pathway of good works than I was as a young ministry wife. But I no longer depend on my good works or fret over what I am not—at least I usually don't. He has shown himself faithful to complete the work He began in me, and I have all the faith in the world that He will complete the work He has begun in you. Love God who sees what you will become. Love yourself because you are in the making. By God's grace you will be more and more like Him.

Make it your goal to please Him (2 Corinthians 5:9).

Question your negative thoughts. Sometimes the expectations or criticisms directed at you are meant to be hurtful, but I believe most of the time they are not. When you feel hurt by a comment about your motive—"I wonder how much she paid for those shoes!"—question your negative interpretation of the words. Maybe the speaker is genuinely curious. Maybe she is considering a pair just like those. Even when you choose to ascribe the better motive and find you are wrong, most of the time you will be right.

The discipline or "practiced habituation" part is to continually question the nature of the negative comment. Choose to believe that most of the comments are not meant to be hurtful. Making this choice is easier for women who have a strong sense of self and a strong view of God's love and grace. It's a practice that has served me well, and I cannot overemphasize the benefits.

Expectations in themselves are not destructive, nor are they instructive. We choose to make them one or the other. **Gain what is helpful from each criticism or expectation.** Ask yourself if there is some grain of truth in this criticism that needs to be examined and used to change a perspective or behavior. This is not berating yourself or demeaning your gifts, rather it is inspecting the fruit of your life. Expectations can be a positive force to shape you toward godliness.

For me, a better practice when faced with a potential hurt has been to ask myself if there is a lesson I need to learn and, if so, determine what it is and how I can improve my attitude. I can say that I am a better person for some of the criticisms I have faced and dealt with.

Continue to treat those who criticize you with love and grace, so they can see that what they said has not changed your love for them. This may be difficult if you are deeply wounded by their comments or have been unjustly attacked. Many times, when I have responded in kindness rather than anger, I have seen the one who attacked me later chastised by God and return to apologize. Proverbs 15:1 says, "A gentle answer turns away wrath."

I was with my husband who was returning a defective toy he had purchased as a Christmas gift and was in deep conversation with the salesman who was completing the return process. The salesman was frustrated by the time-consuming task. John was quietly explaining his situation, and the salesman's annoyance was obviously growing.

Finally, just before the salesman seemed ready to erupt, John said gently, "I realize this is a frustrating experience for you, and there are several people behind me who need your attention, but I appreciate your careful attention. You have spent so much time on this, and I value your help."

The salesman melted; his body lost its angry posture, his face relaxed, and he actually smiled. I was amazed. I was ready to take a swipe at the man for what I perceived was his arrogance in the face of his company's failure to deliver a functional toy. Yet my husband turned the whole situation around 180 degrees with a kind answer.

Help your congregants understand the difference between commitment and competence. They may think you are not contributing to the music because you are not committed, when, in fact, you may not be competent in that area. Maybe you play the piano a little by ear, but it is sometimes difficult to explain to people that playing a little by ear does not qualify you to accompany the choir, which requires extensive sight reading of complex music. It's not lack of commitment that holds you back; it's lack of competence.

Keep your sense of humor. After studying the advice of thousands of ministry wives, Douglas advises them to make an adjustment to the expectations of others.

Such an adjustment, which apparently takes a delicate balance of commitment with detachment and humor, requires separating seriousness about the Gospel from seriousness about yourself, accepting not only God's power and love but also your own finiteness and humanity. For, unless a ministry wife learns how to "ride easy in the saddle of life," she is soon thrown by the multiple situations with which she must cope.[8]

Just love your people. Women who have rarely experienced discouragement in ministry most often suggest that we love our people and surrender our expectations to God. This is easier for those whose personalities are more like Mary than Martha, but it is a lifelong surrender for many of us who are more like Martha. Love your people in spite of their weaknesses and faults, just as you would have them love you in spite of your failures.

God is able to place in your heart the love for Him and His flock that is sufficient to bring His kingdom work into your church.

The second most frequently expressed cause for discouragement is loneliness. We'll address this challenge in the next chapter.

■ FOR YOUR CONSIDERATION

1. What do you think the average churchgoer expects of the minister's wife?
2. What do you think is your most important gift to your congregation?
3. What do you struggle with most—what others expect of you or what you expect of others?

SIX

Loneliness

$\mathcal{I}$ was gathering my books and papers after a lecture I had given one afternoon in a room on the campus of Africa Nazarene University when I noticed a student lingering near the doorway. I had borrowed a heavy projector from the library building to use in the lecture, and he asked if he could carry the projector for me to return it to the library building. On the short walk, the following conversation unfolded.

"What do you like most about Kenya?" he began.

I considered that a few seconds, then spoke with conviction, "The people here are so friendly and kind."

He must have considered these sentiments on other occasions, because his response reflected a well-thought-out question.

"How come you think we are so friendly? Are people in America so mean and unkind to each other that we seem nice in comparison?" His angular, dark face was expressive; something between a skeptical glance and a shy grin rose up.

I walked, clarifying my reflections before I responded. "I think it's something like this. In America, a man is given a task at work, say, making five doors for his door company. He knows he is expected to produce those five doors with efficiency and skill. They are to be as perfect as quality control can make them, without a flaw. He is motivated by the good salary he is receiving, by the pressure to keep his job, and by the pride he holds in his work. By midmorning he has completed two doors, and before lunch he wants to be ready to paint his third door. In the corner of his eye he sees a member of his team hurrying in his direction. He hopes the interaction he sees coming will be brief and uncomplicated. This is an interruption he doesn't need.

"Now consider what happens in Kenya. A man is assigned to work on doors. The deadlines are not clear and the work should be done as carefully as an average man can do it under the circumstances and with the tools that are available. About midmorning, a coworker saunters in to get a tool he cannot find in his workplace. The African man sees a rich and enjoyable conversation ahead with his coworker. He smiles at the opportunity to catch up with his friend's family news. He welcomes the coworker with kind words and a warm smile.

"The business community in America supports the person who is task-oriented, goal-driven, financially yoked. Too often we view the related briskness with its accompanying isolation as a price we must pay for our productivity and convenience lifestyle. So this pressure toward insulation, this aloneness, is almost unavoidable. We must get things done!"

He smiled slowly. We entered the library building where he deposited the projector and we parted after my polite words of gratitude.

Loneliness is all around us, in the cashier at the drugstore who actually tells you how she is when you ask, in the young mother of three who has not had an uninterrupted adult conversation all week, and in the single elementary school teacher who comes home to an empty house. It's here in abundance. There has been much written and said about it. However, there are unique circumstances that drive a debilitating kind of loneliness in the parsonage. This chapter will work to focus on the distinctive factors in the life of the ministry wife that contribute to the form that loneliness takes among us.

Defining the Problem

We need friends. Wendy Murray Zoba, ministry wife and author of a *Christianity Today* article titled "What Pastors' Wives Wish Their Churches Knew," emphasizes three ingredients needed for the health and wholeness of the ministry wife: "clear and healthy attitudes within the congregation, trusted friendships, and a solid relationship with her husband."[1]

Loneliness comes in at least two different stripes. One is common to all women; the other is more frequent among ministry wives. The first, found in most women, stems from a lack of close friends and support networks. It is more widespread among ministry wives who, by choice or need, have refrained from making friends among women of their closest affiliation, the church. Valeriano's ministry wives survey results reported in *Leadership* indicated that fifty-six percent of ministry wives had no close friends in their church; a circumstance perceived by them as their single biggest problem. In twenty-eight percent of these women the choice to avoid making friends in the church was intentional for many reasons, which will be discussed later.[2]

The second type of loneliness is lack of contact time with one's spouse and family, a circumstance that is common to many professionals' spouses but is more complex among ministry wives.

There is a complex balance to be negotiated between inter-dependence and overdependence on one's spouse. If a woman attempts to satisfy her need for companionship by increasing the demand for intimacy from her husband, she may encounter great frustration. He should be, and often is, her main source for encouragement, but he cannot be her only source. In my survey I asked women to name the person or thing that encourages them most, and the number one answer was "my husband."

When asked what helps them most when they experience discouragement, dysthymia, or depression—after spiritual solutions such as prayer and devotional time—women answered "my husband." This is as it should be. It isn't always that way, but it should be. That said, we need friends other than our husbands.

Mary LaGrand Bouma, ministry wife, mother of four, and homemaker of the year for *Family Circle* magazine, gives two reasons why women need women friends. First, it relieves pressure on their marriages. Second, it is nearly impossible for a man, no matter how seasoned he may be, to develop the type of empathy for a woman that another woman can have. Let's face it, men are sometimes clueless about us. A husband is meant to be a companion not a contentment.[3]

Looking at the Data

Half of all the respondents in all the surveys experience loneliness or friendlessness. "No single issue has elicited such powerful and pain-filled remarks from pastors' wives."[4]

Crow's survey found almost half of his respondents feel the need of a trusted friend. The percentage of women who agree with the statement "I have no personal friends for support" remains about thirty percent in all age-groups of ministry wives.

Agreement declines as the tenure of ministry in a particular church increases. It also declines as the size of the church increases and as the amount of education increases. Women in larger churches who are older and have more education have more often acquired friends.[5]

Responses to questions on this subject vary with denomination. In a survey done by Alleman for his dissertation on the "Psychosocial Adjustment of Pastors' Wives," he noted that wives in certain more mainline denominations, such as Presbyterian and United Methodist, were more likely to develop friendships within their congregations. Ministry wives in the Assemblies of God churches were least likely.[6]

Answers vary about where friends can be found. About one-half of all those surveyed by Douglas found friends outside of the church or neighborhood.

Even when there are friends in the church, there is some reticence in these relationships. Of the eighty percent having friends in their congregation, almost one-half felt some lack of freedom in those relationships for many reasons.[7]

Also of interest, even though at any age thirty percent have a trusted friend, it appears that the older you get the less is your felt *need* for a trusted friend. It's the same for tenure in the church; the longer you are there the less you feel the *need* for a trusted friend. Things seem to get better with age and with longevity in a church.

Having children at home increases the felt need for trusted friends and support groups. Thirty-two percent of women without children feel this need. Fifty percent of those with children feel this need.[8]

The "very satisfied" ministry wives accept lonely nights and set-apartness as part of the job and agree that they have many acquaintances but few friends.[9]

Bottom line, loneliness and friendlessness haunt most ministry wives at some time in their lives, more so when young than old, more so when new in a church than when they have had long tenure in a church, more so in some denominations than others, more so in women with children, and less so for college-educated women. Friends are more often found either in the congregation or among clergy wives of the same denomination. Loneliness to some degree comes with the territory.

Reasons for the Problem

For some women, denying close friendships within the congregation is a choice. The women of Alleman's survey indicate two reasons why they chose not to have close friends in the church. First, it was felt that these friendships could create the perception that there are favorites, could generate jealousy, and could produce cliques. Second, the transparency that accompanies close friendships could expose a leader to negative consequences if a trust is violated. It is risky to open up to congregants, but there are signs to help you discover who is trustworthy and who is not. If a woman reveals private information about others to you, be assured she will share those kinds of things about you to others.[10]

Sometimes we choose to deny friendships in the church because we fear a repeat of negative experiences we have had in the past. I admit that I still have lingering disquiet from a painful time in my life.

During my husband's tenure as a youth pastor, a young and very troubled divorcee entered our lives in the hope that she could resolve some deep-seated pain she was enduring. In retrospect, we had little experience with counseling and with maintaining appropriate boundaries and tough love, so we should have referred her to professional help. But we felt as though she needed our help and that God had placed her in our lives for reasons not yet clear to us, so we began to counsel and come alongside her.

In her great need she became overly dependent on us for her mental health, and it was soon apparent that she would not respect our privacy, that she would not listen to our counsel, and that we did not have the skills to help her. Our entanglement became painful. Eventually she moved away, and the sting left from that experience has made me, even now, reluctant to feel safe around women in great psychological need.

Roy M. Oswald, in his article "Why Do Clergy Wives Burn Out?" says something that comes as no surprise to any of us. Loneliness results when there is no one providing pastoral care to the pastor's wife. If her husband thinks he can do this, he is probably guilty of self-deception. If she resorts to some troublesome or improper form of escape, like overmedicating herself, to whom can she confide if she needs help or support?[11]

She feels her husband's job would be in jeopardy if she complained to someone in authority over him. She cannot turn to the members of the church. She might very well undercut her husband's ministry to that congregation. Even if she makes a less than judicious selection of a counselor or therapist, and word of her improper behavior or attitudes get out, she can still damage their ministry in the community. For the most part, she has to swallow her problem. She feels she has no safe place where she can be herself.

A safe place for her rarely develops in the church as a whole, but can exist within a trusted group of church women. Developing such a place often takes time and hard work. Doing so is a developmental process and requires regular attention. Since most ministers move regularly, each may find that after having developed the support that allows her to flourish, she must move to a new community. It takes about four or five years to develop such a support network. In each new setting she may feel the emotional work is not worth the effort.

In many cases, women are lonely because they are told to refrain from making close friends in the church. As the wife of a very young and inexperienced youth pastor, I was advised to avoid close relationships among the congregants of our church. I soon found it curious that those who gave this advice failed to practice what they preached. Nevertheless, in my naiveté I carefully followed their advice until I came to understand that ministry is relational. Some people, by the nature of their circumstances or because of common or shared goals, enter your life more often, understand your heart better, and are more receptive to your support and advice. To construct an artificial barrier to close connections with such people is contrary to the law of love outlined in Corinthians.

The close, personal relationships I have had with a few sterling friends in my church have been my rescue—my release—on many occasions, nor have I suffered fallout from jealous parishioners or those bound to find fault. My spiritual development has been incalculably strengthened as these women commit to pray for me and hold me accountable for spiritual maturity. They have taught me to be a better follower as I watch their commitment to Christ flourish and challenge my own.

They offer us depth and insight as we tune our ears to discover the significance of their lives. The wonderful insights they are ready to teach us about godliness and spiritual reality can be learned around their tables, in hearing their prayer petitions as we pray together, or by sitting on their front steps. Who would want to detach themselves from such richness?[12]

Lorna Dobson, author of *I'm More than the Pastor's Wife,* suggests dealing with the sins of others brings loneliness. When people we love and care for fall spiritually, we find ourselves isolated from them as they withdraw from church and from our circle. We discover in our need for confidentiality that we must to some degree withhold the pain of this loss from others because the burden we carry for the backslider sometimes cannot be shared.[13]

Ruth Senter, speaker, author, and editor of *Partnership,* a magazine for ministry wives, describes this state of loneliness as having the outer noise of busyness but inner sounds of silence.[14] On Sundays and during much of the week we are surrounded by people, but often close to no one. Unfortunately, we sometimes give others the impression that we are too busy to embrace intimacy or tolerate unwanted dependence by others or are too prideful to admit that we really do need people.

Spending time alone is helpful when you like yourself. "I think loneliness is a result of not liking ourselves more than it is of not having people around us."[15] This makes an interesting thought to ponder.

We are regularly viewed as counselors, though often unqualified by training or disposition. We are expected to be skilled listeners, fountainheads of wisdom and spiritual insight, and repositories of information sometimes withheld even from public authorities. Being an unwilling receiver can be lonely.

Saying "How can I help you?" when you really mean "I need help!" can be arduous, draining, and drive us deeper into loneliness.

Loneliness is suffering that comes from lack of intimacy with others, particularly other women. We are disconnected and increasingly more independent in our mobile society. Elizabeth Gilbert, in her book *Committed: A Skeptic Makes Peace with Marriage,* was forced to watch as the love of her life was deported from the United States. In an effort to stand by her man, she chose to live with him in places around the world while they awaited the approval for a marriage license that would then permit him to reside in the States. She stayed for a time in a small, isolated village in northern Vietnam. She decided to study marriage as it is understood among the Hmong people of the village. She was befriended by a tiny, black-haired, twelve-year-old girl who spoke remarkable English and served as a translator.

Aside from the interesting details of the actual marriage ceremony, Elizabeth described life in the village. Large, extended families lived together, and "women's work" kept women in constant touch with each other. She asked a question of the village women about loneliness, then went on to describe the curious bafflement expressed by these women when they were confronted with the concept of loneliness. Apparently it was not well understood in this culture, and for good reason. There was no lack of intimacy among the women.[16]

In our ever smaller, ever more nuclear, insulated family structure, one or two people have become the source of our too concentrated social interactions and expectations. In larger social units like tribes or closely living extended families, the expectations for support and comfort are spread among many family members. Women just naturally, because of proximity, become the social contact and fulfill the need in women for human interaction. Because the social unit of our society is a single, often isolated family with two or three or possibly four members, the same number of expectations is imposed on a small clutch of family members.

Childless couples, or husbands and wives in the days preceding the birth of their children, sometimes expect the spouse to bear the majority of expectations for social contact. He or she must often be the sole—or at least the primary—support, the confidant, the sounding board, the comforter, the strong arm, the listener, the intellectual equal, and the list goes on. Thus isolated in our family units, we place all these expectations on our spouse, and the result is that he fulfills less and less of our needs, we become more and more disillusioned, and as one consequence we are convinced he is not the man we hoped he would be.

The United States as a whole retains an enormously high divorce rate for complex reasons, but this disillusionment contributes to it. In societies like the Hmong of Vietnam, a woman marries and from the husband there is financial support, procreation, maybe even love, but the expectations for support are so spread among other women, mothers, grannies, aunties, and female siblings that husband-expectations are lowered and this parallels the lower divorce rate. Women know each other and work in such closely aligned tasks that talk and intimacy are natural.

Even in our workplaces where there is a demand for contact, we are lonely because there is no need for intimacy in the contact. In Ken Crow's NEA study, forty-four percent of pastors' wives respond positively to the statement "my current need is for a trusted friend" regardless of whether or not they have full-time jobs.[17] One way to interpret this data is to suggest that even though their jobs are providing contact, there is no more intimacy at work than at any other place.

Here is a list of intimacy stealers, as Carol Kent identifies them:

- Viewing ourselves as unlovable.
- Having unrealistic expectations of someone else. You will have to release your vision of the ideal friend of your dreams.
- Being too busy. You may be substituting busyness for intimacy. You may need to let some things go for the rewards of intimacy with a friend.
- Struggling with poor communication skills.[18]

Types of Loneliness

Paul Tournier dissects loneliness into two categories, the fruitful kind and the tragic kind. The fruitful kind stems from a position of choice. You choose solitude that you might gain insight and the solitude results in a type of fruitful loneliness. This is the kind of loneliness Christ must have endured during his forty days in the wilderness. It was chosen for a greater good. The second kind of fruitful loneliness is that which stems from a choice to stand courageously alone to defend a truth.[19]

I have known people who stood alone against abortion in a room full of angry people. I have on occasion felt the need to stop the progress of gossip among a group of women. In the process of attempts to graciously arrest the discussion, I have felt alone. That kind of loneliness has a measure of choice behind it. It is fruitful because it advances a cause, stops an injustice, or brings it into focus.

The tragic kind of loneliness can, in fact, be fruitful but often only in retrospect and sometimes not at all. London and Wiseman call it self-induced loneliness, the kind that comes when we refuse to be known or let anyone into our inner world. It is a choice, but one loaded with pressure from within that can obscure the notion that we *have* a choice. It is common to ministry wives who think no one outside the ministry could understand their problem; that women in the church should not be allowed into their hearts for whatever reason, that those in authority cannot be trusted with their story because of possible negative ramifications if it is exposed.

These women are often afraid to reach out to let anyone close. They withdraw from the care of others who might bring consolation or comfort. Often members of the congregation perceive this behavior as one chosen by their ministry wife because she needs privacy. "You can clutch privacy so closely to your chest that it closes your heart from welcoming those who love you the most."[20]

When I see lonely women who are convinced they cannot have friends, I think of Jesus with his twelve close friends. Three of them were his sterling friends. Were there problems of jealousy and betrayal? Yes. But even on the night before His crucifixion, He gathered all of them for an intimate chat about the future and about His fears. Eventually, those He nurtured in friendship brought the gospel to the world. Not all of them, but most did. The rewards were worth the risks.

Another kind of tragic loneliness springs from living at great distances from family and home communities. This type is often through no free choice of our own. This occurs when God has opened up a church or a place of service in another region of the country or the world. Since most couples in ministry move frequently, it is common for women to be far from family and home. This is especially painful if they were raised in or expect to remain close to a loving, connected family.

Dealing with the Problem

I love the analogy Thomas Oord and Michael Lodahl use in their book *Relational Holiness* when explaining how God and humankind interact to live out His calling in our lives. They propose that the living relationship we have with God is a dance, a soul-salsa, if you will. God is the leader, we follow Him, yet we must consent to dance, to be led and in fact to contribute to the graceful steps whose outcome is beautiful, coordinated, joyful, and satisfying. As life becomes more complex, the dance becomes more intricate, exquisite with no end to the elegant variations that are displayed as we interact with God.[21]

Managing loneliness is one of those complexities. It can contribute to the exquisite variations on the theme as we learn to adjust, to respond to the pressures of the Holy Spirit, the small whispers of God. The learning process is sometimes awkward, difficult, requiring repeated commitments to the practice of it, but the results are a powerful, glorious, beautiful testimony of God's grace.

What are the steps? How do we practice this dance? Here are some suggestions from other ministry wives gleaned from their experiences and from mine.

Make the effort to cultivate a friend and to be a friend. Stop wishing things were different and do what you can to make them different. You will probably need to take the initiative. For those of us whose personality flourishes in the company of friends, press past your pain or reluctance or fear of rejection or criticism. Try to make a friend. Be advised that some ministry wives are quite content with a best friend husband or an aloneness they cherish. Although Valeriano's data suggest that fifty-six percent of ministry wives do not have a close friend in the church, forty-four percent do.[22] Those of us who do, think it is worth the risk. If that's too scary, and you need a friend, make one outside the church.

Pray for God to send you a friend. She may already be there. Examine your present relationships for potential. But be careful not to view this process as though you were looking for people to award with your friendship. This might be good for your ego, but it smacks of arrogance and pride.

Begin your search with a good conversation to determine if the person you are connecting with is a good candidate for a close friend. A satisfying conversation with a friend looks something like the give and take of a game of volleyball. Team A has the ball for a period of time and everyone on both teams is focused on the ball. They do not pursue their own thoughts or consider how they should have completed a play in the first quarter. They do not study the net or the uniforms of their teammates. They do not ruminate over the championship game they played in the last season nor do they reflect on any slight injury suffered from a fall in the preceding game. They keep thoroughly focused on the ball in court A and where it is going. Soon the ball is sent to team B where, again, all the members of both teams focus on the ball in team B's court.

Conversations between good friends begin with friend A speaking her mind, expressing her ideas while friend B is fully focused on friend A's thoughts and ideas. Friend B, in an effort to clearly understand where the ball is and what it can do, will clarify, ask questions related to friend A's concerns, and generally attempts to fully understand friend A. In an ideal friendship, friend A will wind down and pass the conversation to friend B. Friend A will be fully engaged in the topic of friend B, will clarify and ask questions and make appropriate sounds of commiseration until friend B has been clearly understood and the process repeats itself.

I sat at a table during a wedding reception recently and had a conversation with a man who clearly did not understand this volleyball model principle. He spoke continuously for forty-five minutes about the accomplishments of his children. To be honest, I enjoyed hearing about his children; they were close to my children while they were growing up, and I enjoy keeping up with their exploits. But in true friend fashion, I think he should have been interested in my family as well.

I attempted a firm but futile effort to get the ball passed into my court, but he would not budge. He would have the ball for the entire game. I wanted to ask him how long he thought an audience would remain engaged in a volleyball game if one team had the ball for the entire game. I was sorely tempted to advise him about the volleyball game model of conversation, but truthfully, I am certain it would not have altered his behavior in the least.

Good friends know that conversations must be shared and must have focus from both parties. If you want a good friend because you need someone to talk to, remember you must be a friend and expect to be a great listener as well.

Having advocated for trusted friends, there is a caution that surfaces from my experience and that of many ministry women. "Share your heart but use your head."[23] Guard your tongue about other people in the church. Even among close, intimate friends, there are boundaries that should be respected, confidences that should be kept. If you have information that will cause church division or constitutes gossip, ask yourself, *Is it better for me to feel the relief of a burden shared, or is it better to leave this unsaid and assure that the unity of the church is preserved?* Ecclesiastes 3:7 veritably shouts that there is "a time to be silent and a time to speak," even among very close friends.

Keep to yourself any little annoyances about your husband that might interfere with someone's hearing the truth from him as he preaches.

It's that dance with God again. You give a gentle push or tug, He responds with restraint or release. It works best if you are very familiar with His signals. The older you get, and as you grow in the knowledge of Christ, the better you know them.

Being unable to express some of your heaviness or to release a hurt to a friend because of the confidential nature of the problem may leave you with a residual loneliness that for some is very difficult to bear. Kathy Slamp, ministry wife, author, and speaker, explains this residual loneliness:

> There remains an isolation and loneliness that comes from being set apart—there are no two ways about it. In our case, these feelings have brought my husband and me together in a unique bond that is only enhanced by the separation created by his calling. It's not a curse; it's just the way things are. At this point in the journey, I couldn't think of a life I would like better. Keeping that lip zipped doesn't rob me of my individuality, and it doesn't inhibit my lifestyle. But it's a vital lesson we learn early on that protects us and keeps us above the fray.[24]

Before going any further, let me address the longstanding argument that we should not have friends in the church because it causes jealousies, cliques, and so forth. Pardon me if

I say this is bunk. There are successful ways of handling close friendships in the church.

I think what this statement really translates into is, don't be exclusive in your attention to certain people in your church. Be friendly to everyone at church and at church functions. My close friends at church do not need to sit with me at any given church supper. They don't need to monopolize my conversations at the end of the service. We are not dependent on each other's attention but are free in any setting to give our attention to whomever we choose, secure in the knowledge that we will take time to connect at some point regularly at lunch or over tea. We e-mail and call, but corporate time is for us to mingle with everyone.

Proverbs 18:24 (KJV) indicates a person who wants friends must be friendly. Reach out. You may find your first few attempts unsuccessful, but keep trying. Don't be in a hurry. Above all, don't quit. The process takes time.

Here's some general advice about developing friends from the perspective of ministry women who have written on this subject.

Avoid getting close to women who are contentious. Be comfortable with women of all ages. Choose friends who support their husbands, pray for their children, hunger for God, and have a servant spirit.[25]

Be wise in choosing friends and take time to cultivate friendships. Have a common purpose with them. Value them, rally behind them as a member of a team. Jesus lived with His friends, the ones He wanted to influence most, the ones from whom He requested prayer. He even had some very special friends in the church (Peter, James, and John) and outside the church (Mary, Martha, and Lazarus). Having close friends is biblical, even for those in ministry. Don't be exclusive in church settings, but do let others see you enjoying your friends. Some friends will be for a season, some for a lifetime. The value of having a relationship should outweigh the risks. View your husband as your best friend and never let any other relationship come between or above this.[26]

During a difficult period in her ministry, and under the pressure of a senior pastor's wife to refrain from making friendships in the church, Jill Briscoe found herself lonely and in need of a friend. She sat at her kitchen table and considered the friendships of Christ. She drew five concentric circles that represented the levels of friendships that Christ had and filled the circles with numbers. The outer circle she marked "multitudes." The next, inner concentric circle had the word "seventy" written in it, representing Jesus' close acquaintances. The third circle indicated the twelve disciples. The fourth circle, the three— James, John, and Peter. The innermost circle had one.

She prayed and asked God which individuals in her life belonged in what circles. She wrote the names of people she knew in the circles of her life. "As I wrote names in those circles I finally quit feeling guilty about having friends—about not spending as much time with my 'seventy' as I spent with my 'twelve,' or as much time with the 'twelve' as I did with my 'three,' and so on. As I was freed up to pursue friendships, many needs were met, and I was enabled to be a better—and less stressed— youth worker's wife."[27]

"He who loves a pure heart and whose speech is gracious will have the king for his friend" (Proverbs 22:11). If you find that in a developing relationship you are asked to be a sounding board for someone whose words are not gracious, who is a gossip, or who complains about a third party, ask yourself if this is a relationship worth pursuing. Better still, respond like Frances Simpson, veteran ministry wife. "I remember another lady who called us often to talk about the shortcomings of a 'friend' of hers. Finally, one day when she called, I believe it was the Lord who inspired me to say, 'Evidently our friend is having a hard time right now. Let's pray for her.' I began to pray for both of them. She never called to complain about the other lady again."[28]

"Perfume and incense bring joy to the heart, and the pleasantness of one's friend springs from his earnest counsel" (Proverbs 27:9). Good guidance for defining what makes a friend pleasant to be with.

Being a friend can mean developing a humble spirit. We need not be the admired authority. As ministry spouses we are often placed on pedestals in the minds of our parishioners. Some of us are very uncomfortable there, while others like the feeling and work to perpetuate the notion that we are a cut above. This counteracts friendship. People feel uncomfortable around those who continually seem to know it all. Walk among the women of your church as a servant (1 Peter 5:1-3). Shepherd God's people, and be an example in your walk.

Consider investing in a friendship with another ministry wife, either one within your denomination or one within another denomination. One woman in Florida started a group especially for ministry wives. They meet once a month for fellowship, study, and prayer. Another group of ministry wives have vowed to meet just for fun. They shop, play golf, go to baseball games, and have tea. The point is to meet with women who have common life challenges. You need to talk to each other. It is refreshing to see that others experience the same challenges you do. Besides, in expressing what you feel to them, you will probably discover the humor in it and laugh together. Laughter is a great medicine. I heard it once said that a good belly laugh is equal to three tablespoons of oat bran.

Perhaps you have attempted to develop a friendship with someone and have felt there is no reciprocal effort from her and you seem to be doing all the work. Carol Kent describes the frustration experienced by Kate, a woman seeking to develop a friend, Ann, in her book *Secret Passions of the Christian Woman*. The reasons for this frustration are complex and beautifully identified in chapter 7 of her book. It's a great study in understanding interpersonal relationships. She describes all the elements involved in an ideal intimate relationship that she would enjoy and then explains where some of these elements are mismatched or misunderstood in the communication between Kate and Ann.[29]

For example, Kate needed frequent time and reassurance of the connection with her friend. Ann valued her privacy and needed solitude. Kate wanted an accountability partner, but Ann was less vocal and more reserved; so Kate's advances in this area were not reciprocated. Eventually Kate went through four women in her attempt to develop close companionship. Understanding yourself, controlling your expectations, and seeking God's timing are important in this process.

Disciple other women. In my survey, I asked women who rarely get discouraged about ministry what advice they could give to others. Often repeated were the sentiments, "Help people who need help, and you will not be alone." The more we give ourselves away, the richer and more satisfying life becomes. If you bring joy to someone, joy will return to you. Love begets love. It has been said that the only love you get to keep is the love you give away.

Count on God. Grow every part of your life with prayer and experiences with God. In time you may be able to see that deep incisions such as loneliness are a means of self-understanding. You may continue to feel alone, but remember you never are alone. For God has promised to "never leave you nor forsake you" (Hebrews 13:5, NKJV).

Elisabeth Elliot once spoke in a nearby church, and I had the privilege of hearing her describe her experiences of loneliness. She was then married to her third husband and had experienced the death of both her previous husbands. The loneliness that follows such losses is beyond my imagining and to know its dark coldness twice could leave a shell of scars hard to overcome. She shares these experiences:

> Loneliness comes over us sometimes as a sudden tide. It is one of the terms of our humanness, and, in a sense, therefore, incurable. Yet I have found peace in my loneliest times not only through acceptance of the situation, but through making it an offering to God, who can transfigure it into something for the good of others.[30]

Pray and cooperate with His whispers. Reach out and take a risk and listen for God's voice. Learn to feel His presence through His Word. This comes through the personal relationship we have with God. This is the way we dance with Him.

Realize that some loneliness stems from our thought processes. In this case you can think your way out of the dark place, just as you thought your way there. It starts like this, *It's my birthday and no one has called or sent me a thoughtful note celebrating my special day. It's because no one appreciates me or loves me for who I am. After all I have done for this church, you would think someone would remember my birthday.*

Think again. *To be honest, I may have neglected the celebration of others on their birthdays. I find it so easy to forget, I will forgive those who have also forgotten. Next time my friend's birthday comes around I will give her a call. Let me put that on my calendar right now.*

Truth be told, when you wonder where He is in your loneliness, He is in the kindness of your neighbor who agrees to watch your children when you need to go to the doctor. He is in the heart of the oldest woman in your church who baked a pie for you as you entertained the missionary. He is in the card you received from a member of your Sunday School class. If you are blessed, He will be in the sterling friend who listens, who will share her grief with you, who will erupt in laughter at a funny story she relays to cheer you up on a gloomy Monday. Friends are God's way of entering your loneliness. Developing them is work but worth the effort, the time, and the risk. This effort is the way we dance with God.

Ever feel like a single parent who is managing life with an absentee husband? Take a look at what ministry wives say in the next chapter helps them in this frustrating problem.

■ FOR YOUR CONSIDERATION

1. If you have been unsuccessful in developing a trusted friend, ask God to help you understand why. Can you articulate any reasons you think might explain this?

2. Do you find yourself identifying with a scenario in this chapter? Why?

3. Make a list of qualities you would like to see in an ideal friend. Consider which ones you may need to compromise on with a friendship you may be developing.

4. Draw a circle like Jill Briscoe did, then four more concentric circles within it. Fill the outer circle with the word *many*, the second circle in with the number of people you connect with on any given Sunday. Pray and ask God to help you place the names of people in each of the remaining circles in the manner Jill did. Take a few days to think and pray about this until you have a well-thought-out and prayed-over list of potential close friends. Ask God to help you proceed in establishing better friendships with these women.

SEVEN

Your Husband's Schedule

Married love does not consist of gazing at each other, but of looking outward together in the same direction. **(Anonymous)**

 can imagine she sat at the cramped desk in the corner of her kitchen and typed from her heart of the frustration she felt in her role as a ministry wife:

> *I really need some help here. I am seriously think-ing about leaving my husband who also happens to be my pastor. It seems like now that he's pastoring that we never have time together and he spends most of his time at the church. When I want us to do things together we always have to cancel our plans because of church stuff. When he's home I can't even have a decent conversa-tion with him. We can sit in the same room for hours and hours and not say one word. If I try to touch him or anything like that he says, stop/quit. I am sick of it because I can be miserable by myself. Also he can pray fire and brimstone for someone else but we never pray or study together. Anything that we do like that is done separately. I am tired of living the lie and I want out.*[1]

The church congregation can feel like a domineering mistress whose pressure to abstain from all other interests or obligations is too strong to resist. In some studies the husbands' time with family is of primary concern to ministry wives.

Defining the Problem

Although the above quote is from a pastor's wife, much of it could very well have sprung from the heart of the wife of an on-call doctor, traveling salesman, attorney whose night court visits are increasing, policeman whose life is on-call 24/7, soldier, army commander, or superintendent of schools in a small community. I spoke recently to Bill Hays, a teacher in the education department who spent dozens of years as a superintendent of schools in a nearby village. When I described what I was trying to say in this chapter, he suggested I talk to his wife about how much his profession demanded of her. Apparently, she was required to tolerate lack of husband time often during any given week. Issues surrounding a husband's or wife's lack of time at home are common today among professional workers.

Besides not being physically present, pastors can sometimes be mentally absent. There are several reasons why men in ministry are less attentive at home than most of us might wish. Giving focused attention to people's problems is a draining occupation. If he is out giving his full focus to those in the hospital or in a nursing home or to families in crisis, he may return home drained of his ability to listen. This type of psychological drain does not occur so often among those who do manual labor or whose work does not involve great interpersonal focus. Working with people is especially depleting to those who tend to be characterized as introverts. These ministers find themselves "over-peopled" as Roy M. Oswald puts it. If the wife decides to respect his requirement for solitude, she may find she has to swallow her own needs. This puts a strain on her and makes her feel as though she is competing with church for his attention. Oswald further suggests that the minister may be tempted to become a workaholic because he finds work, with its adoring public, more enjoyable than home with the criticism or guilt he experiences there.[2]

To compound the problem, the ministry wife feels guilty about questioning the time he spends in church duties because she may feel she is expecting him to compromise God's work to fulfill her needs. After all, isn't he supposed to be the servant who forsakes all to follow God? If she believes in his call, it is harder to protect her boundaries from its demands. Further complicating the matter is the reality that even when he is there, he may not be really there. Phone calls, text messages, and e-mails take priority. His mind may be on tangled church matters or parishioners' intractable problems. She may feel he is spending time with the family out of duty rather than love. She and/or the family come second to everything church-related.[3]

Let's put this in perspective. Most ministry wives may be annoyed, frustrated, or discouraged, but more often than not they see that the overall picture of their lot is still positive. When asked, "On the whole, do you think your husband's being a minister is a benefit or a hazard to your family?" Seventy-four percent indicated it was more of a benefit than a hazard.[4] For these women, the problems were more than compensated for by the rewards of ministry.

That said, the problem needs to be looked at and addressed as a real and compelling issue in the discouragement of ministry wives.

A Look at the Data

Duane Alleman writes in his doctoral dissertation a review of the literature on the subject of pastor overinvolvement.

The church has been likened to a "seductive mistress that demands all a man's interest, time and emotional involvement" (Douglas, 1965, p. 206). The approximately 200 ministers' wives from eight denominations responding to a questionnaire by Corskery (1977) stated that they considered the congregation's demands on their husband's time to be the greatest problem area in their lives. Denton (1961b) similarly found that the lack of family time is what women disliked most about being married to a minister. Sixty-eight percent of the wives in Mace and Mace's study (1980) considered time alone with their husbands to be their greatest need in adjusting to their husband's ministry, while over seventy percent of those surveyed by Watts (1982) were concerned about not having sufficient family time. Unfortunately, the relationship between the minister, his wife, and congregation can form an "emotional triangle" with each vying for, and jealous of, the others' time and attention (Douglas, 1961a).[5]

According to Crow's large, random, NEA study, the concern is greater for women under thirty (forty percent) and declines steadily to seven percent for women over sixty. The concern declines as tenure at a particular church increases, is less if the wife has a full-time job and has at least a college degree, and, as might be expected, declines if there are no children at home.[6]

Managing the Problem

Before suggesting any approaches to the problem, there are some things that should be understood as virtually immutable.

Understand that the pastoral ministry, like many professions, can never be reduced to a forty-hour-a-week job. Like housework, it is never done. Overtime is not a choice; it is expected because the church is often thought of as a family. Medical emergencies, deaths, and crises are not amenable to convenient scheduling.

Because of the nature of volunteer church work, evenings are often the only times that are free for members of the congregation. More and more of them work during the day and can conduct the business of the church or any volunteer work only during the evenings and on weekends.

Start with God. One ministry wife relayed this story that illustrates the first way to address this problem. She describes her disappointment at the continued absence of her husband in their early years of ministry and her awareness that God was asking her to examine her attitudes on the subject. As a result of these promptings, she began a more intimate journey with God. When she had a longing for more of her husband, she began to go to God first rather than to her husband. When she felt hurt or neglected, she turned her wounded heart to God and asked Him to be her deliverer. She began to dialogue with Him, to cherish His words, and through them He counseled her. As she became more secure in her dependence on God, she became less clingy with her husband. The change in their relationship took place over a period of several years. By then she no longer looked to her husband to fulfill all her companionship needs, but rather she looked first to God, in whom we "have been made complete" according to Colossians 2:10 (NASB). The prophet Jeremiah seems to indicate that when we trust in someone else to give us what only God can give us, we live under a curse (Jeremiah 17:5-8).

This dependence on God made her more attractive to her husband. He began to see her as a support rather than a distraction whose sad face or tears depleted him whenever he left for a church duty. It was during this time that their romance began to flourish. She saw his love as the icing on the cake, not the cake. Intimacy with God was the cake. When she stopped demanding so much intimacy from her husband and discovered intimacy with God she became whole, which led to greater intimacy with her husband.

Love and accept him in spite of his propensity to overwork or be less than you think he should be. He is not perfect, and he knows it. How often—and I still can't get past this at times—do I settle into my pew on Sunday morning after our awesome musical worship and sincere prayer offered by our assistant pastor, then start feeling critical of my husband's sermon. *What if he says something that offends our family?* or *The details of that illustration aren't accurate* or *Oh, brother, he's got the man's age wrong* or *Why can't he illustrate what he is talking about?—it's so confusing.*

As I reflect on this now in the quiet of my kitchen this reminds me of times when during an attempt to relay a story to a friend, I cringed as my children corrected my inaccuracies. "It wasn't Wednesday, it was Thursday," or "There were only two tomatoes not three in the basket," or some other insignificant detail. To both my friend and me, these details were wholly unimportant to the content of the story. The point was made regardless if there were two *or* three tomatoes. It's the same with my husband's sermons. The congregation is not hung up on the accuracy of the details of each illustration. They get the point. And really, what they value most is his life illustrating the gospel. I don't need to remind him of his failures, I just need to love him and be proud that he longs to preach God's Word to his congregation, that he has a heart after God, and that his life is a response to God's call, imperfect though that rendering may be.

If he can't be home as many nights as you would like, love him anyway. This is not to say you need to stuff your negative feelings or fail to call his attention to what you see as a serious family problem, but first and foremost he should know you love him unconditionally, in spite of his seeming neglect. There is a time and place for confrontation, but it can be done with grace and respect and, above all, love.

Release your expectations, but don't abandon them. Jan Congo illustrates this release through a story. A ministry wife dreamed she was in an operating room of a hospital. Her husband was on the operating table and Jesus Christ was the surgeon. Jesus said to her, "I am going to use you to help in the surgery and healing of your husband."

She puzzled over this for a few moments then asked, "Lord, what is my role in this surgery? Shall I be the scalpel so that you can cut out the cancerous tumors?" She thought to be a means of changing him, of removing the failings of his life.

Jesus said to her, "No, you shall be the IV to bring him nourishment and health-giving fluids to support his equilibrium." God meant for her to be his consolation not his correction.[7]

I have been guilty, as most women have, of trying to make my husband my renovation project—to "encourage" him to live up to my expectations. Sometimes he needs my advice, but God has designed me primarily to be his support and helpmeet, not his instructor. I admit this is a tough one for me. I am a teacher by choice, training, and nature. I instruct. It's what I do and who I am, and too often he is my class project.

Some of us enter marriage with expectations that may require a lifetime to correct. The adjustment learning curve is steep in the first year of marriage but tapers off to a slow incline that concludes in a level—though somewhat wiggly—line by the time we reach retirement. But we spend that first year trying to figure out who we married. The infatuation curve is slowly declining and genuine, giving love is sometimes only sprouting. Love seems to have the inverse curve of infatuation and the struggle between these two begins its resolution after the honeymoon year.

A married pastor has his own family for a parish. His covenant with his wife and family provides that they are his priority church. God and his congregation are watching how he ministers to his priority church. They need his example. Paul tells us, "The overseer . . . must manage his own family well" (1 Timothy 3:2, 4). He cannot accomplish that if he is an absentee husband and father. By his example he is preaching a sermon more powerful than any that comes from his pulpit on Sunday, because a role model is worth a thousand sermons. Neither a perfect ministry nor a perfect marriage is a requirement for glorifying God, but a listening, obedient heart is. That said, you must remember to release your expectations of him to God.

Don't abandon your expectations, however. He can benefit from your belief that he can be greater than he is. Do let your expectations be refined by God and then continually released to Him. Only He can do the changing. If you try, you may become the "constant dripping on a rainy day" described in Proverbs 27:15. However, you can help the process with your positive reinforcement. Consider this story of positive reinforcement:

A psychology class met in a large lecture hall at the front of which was a central blackboard with a desk on the right and a heater located in the far left corner of the room. Students in the class decided early in the semester to subject the instructor to a simple psychological experiment. When he moved toward the desk they acted uninterested, bored, watched the clock, put their heads on their desks, whispered, and created all manner of distractions. When he moved toward the heater they sat attentively, stayed focused on his words, asked questions, and responded to his questions. By the end of the semester he was sitting on the heater as he lectured.

Tell him when he is doing something right. Tell him often, and see if he moves toward the heater.

In Lorna Dobson's book *I'm More than a Pastor's Wife*, she lists thirty-three ways to give your pastor-husband positive reinforcement. The first way she suggests is to "compliment something in the service within the first ninety minutes afterward: message, illustration, etc."[8] Other suggestions are to communicate to him that you appreciate the things he does that few people see, like praying over a sleeping cancer patient or learning the names of the children of a single mom in the church. Tell him what makes you proud of him.

Choose to view your differences of opinion in a positive light. If you are usually the optimist and he is usually the pessimist, see this as a balance that keeps you both functioning with level, forward steps. If he is meticulous and you are more carefree, this can be a source of irritation, but choose to see it as a way of moving you both toward equilibrium. You and I have seen unmarried women and men who lack the balancing pressure of a mate and are too eccentric to be used of God as fully as they might. Be positive about these balancing pressures from your spouse. You can be negative only so long before you begin to disintegrate.

What if I am trying to improve the situation and nothing is happening? Sometimes when conversations have concluded, you think he has heard and understood you, and you have released your expectations as much as you can, yet there seems to be no response or effort to repair the situation. Following is my advice mixed in with Martie Stowell's, who is cited in the book *The Joy of a Promise Kept: The Powerful Role Wives Play,* and is the wife of the president of Moody Bible Institute.

Examine what you do have control over. You cannot control his actions. If you try he will resent it. You can control your own actions and attitudes. You can choose to be disrespectful, crabby, or silent in an attempt to punish him, or you can choose to be forgiving and talk honestly about how you are feeling. If you choose self-control and forgiveness, your marriage will benefit immeasurably in the long run.

What does this choice look like? First, it uses words for healing rather than for attacking. He needs to know how you feel in a respectful, clear way without attacking him and his faults. If tempers flare, take a break and agree to a time when the conversation can resume under greater self-control.

Second, it is tolerant. John has had to put up with a cargo of arrogance and "instruction" from me regularly. Even as God has for Christ's sake forgiven me, and I would like my husband to forgive me of my shortcomings, I shall forgive him. God is merciful and full of grace, so shall I be.

Third, it uses prayer as a priority. Pray that God would give you wisdom and love and forgiveness. Pray for your husband that he would be clay in God's hands (not your hands).

Martie Stowell continues:

Fourth, it perseveres. Make a concerted but patient, grace-filled effort toward resolution. Don't give up the effort. A successful family is not a family without problems. It is a family that is successfully working on the problems. What are the actions that you can now agree on that need to take place? Do either of you need to apologize?

Are these things accomplished with ease? Not for most of us. But there is grace for us even in this.

When your mind is resolved to move ahead, but your feelings are lingering in the land of anger, bitterness, and jealousy over the competition you feel with the church, hasten to defeat these negative feelings. The advice above can help you make progress, but when these feelings strike unbidden, go to God and pour out your pain. Can you find a confidant to whom you can unburden your heart? If your feelings solidify into destructive thoughts or acts, consider counseling. Be careful not to be envious of another wife who has a "good" husband. Don't flounder in self-pity. And don't allow your feelings to make you into a bitter person.

Your response to your husband when he breaks a promise will have an impact on your marriage. Your goal should be to reflect Jesus Christ who offered forgiveness to those who crucified Him. Love in the face of a broken promise can bring profound healing and unity to your marriage. Your husband will be strengthened and encouraged to see that you still stand by him, even when he blows it, and you will grow in your walk with God. You will be able to say that you have put God's Word into practice in your life.[9]

One caveat; if you, like the woman at the beginning of this chapter who was expressing her desire to leave her husband, have found the situation intolerable, seek professional help. Ask God to lead you to someone who can work with you to resolve these heavy issues. It is not a sign of weakness to ask for help.

The number one solution to the pressures that ministry wives face lies in the next chapter.

■ FOR YOUR CONSIDERATION

1. In what ways are you and your husband opposites? How has that difference helped you be more balanced?

2. If you are an experienced ministry wife, in what ways have you seen God change your expectations of your husband? If you are new in this position, what behaviors of your husband that you think he should change do you find frustrating?

3. Remind yourself of the things he does that make you proud inside. If you can come up with a list of seven, mention one to him in passing each day next week.

EIGHT

Developing Spiritual Reserves

I bring no esoteric cryptogram, no mystic coder to be painfully deciphered. I appeal to no hidden law of the unconscious, no occult knowledge meant only for a few. The secret is an open one which the wayfaring man may read. It is simply the old and ever-new counsel: Acquaint thyself with God. (**A. W. Tozer**)[1]

*T*here is an inner joy that comes to those whose walk has brought them close to the heart of God. Blustering winds of worry seem less and less able to loosen their resolve. They experience calm when there is no reason for it. They "rejoice in the Lord, always," and as the Hebrew word for rejoice indicates, they return to the source of their joy, always. They re-joy. Most of these women have walked with God for a lifetime and hear His voice in the sounds of every day, see His face in the joys of common life. They know a peace that bypasses the mind and goes straight to the heart. They walk with a permanent lean toward the side where Jesus walks with them. They know who they are in Christ, and they rejoice to see God's kingdom increase rather than their own. It is true that most deeply spiritual women have struggles and feel defeated at times. Their testimonies verify this, but in many respects they instruct us in the way of an overcomer.

I have seen snatches of these attributes in women I have known. Barbara, tall, stately, gray-haired, and smiling, makes everyone feel at home in her presence. I can sit beside her at lunch anytime and know I have her undivided attention. Her smile is unruffled. In Marcia's presence I sense spiritual peace that comes through an immense desire to know God. She has developed a life of prayer that leaves me comforted when I give her a prayer request, knowing with certainty that my appeal will be given serious time before the throne of God. My mother lived to serve Christ through others and was in turn loved by them for her caring heart. These women would each give credit to Christ for their development. It is spiritual maturity that gives each of them a bouquet of joy whose aroma reaches out to even the casual bystander.

It is this progress toward God and these spiritual resources that lead to a sacred recess that can carry ministry wives through hard places. Sixty-seven percent of women in my survey who answered the question, "What helps me most during a period of discouragement, dysthymia, or depression?" included some reference to spiritual disciplines: Bible reading, prayer, meditating, trusting God and His faithfulness, fasting, worship, solitude. These are so important that thirty-three percent of the women in the Douglas study said the most important advice they would give to a new ministry wife would be to deepen her personal commitment to Christ and the church.[2]

What are the disciplines that lead to spiritual maturity? What gives us strength in the daylight for power in the darkness? Dallas Willard, in his book *The Spirit of the Disciplines*, listed some of the practices that deepen this walk with God.

- *Disciplines of Abstinence:* Solitude, silence, fasting, frugality, chastity, secrecy, sacrifice

- *Disciplines of Engagement:* Study, worship, celebration, service, prayer, fellowship, confession, submission[3]

Richard Foster, in his book *Celebration of Discipline: The Path to Spiritual Growth,* divides his list into three parts:

- *Inward Disciplines:* meditation, prayer, fasting, study
- *Outward Disciplines:* simplicity, solitude, submission, service
- *Corporate Disciplines:* confession, worship, guidance, celebration[4]

At first glance these appear like exercises for cloistered holy women who are free of the responsibilities of carpools; teaching Sunday School; keeping children fed, clean, and reasonably well behaved; and getting dinner on the table by 5:30 P.M. How can women of enormous responsibility in the church, the parsonage, the family, and the workplace manage such practices? They seem so unreachable, yet if we look closely at the spiritual quarter of our lives, most of us long to be where these disciplines take us. I want to walk with the King so closely that He becomes my peace in all things; that His kingdom plays out in my world as it does in heaven. I am hungry to leave a legacy for Jesus. That's where it begins—being hungry for more of God. As Tozer said, "Acquaint thyself with God."

Many authors offer their suggestions on the subject, but all of their proposals take time. For most of us, the real question is whether we want this enough to give this process the gift of our time. It's a matter of sharpening the saw. We can continue to cut down trees with a dull saw and see limited results, or we can stop our frantic doings to offer our time in worship to the one who crowns our activities with success, thereby sharpening the saw. We can accomplish more kingdom work, develop more inner peace, if we put the time into honing our saw. Sure, there are days and times when these disciplines seem routine and anything but empowering, but they are at work building brick upon brick the foundation onto which the temple of God's work is constructed. The bottom line is, do you want this empowered life *enough?*

God calls us to be champions of His power, but each champion begins his or her journey into history with the mundane. The Olympic skier begins on bunny hills, over and over and over. They listen to trainers; they eat a certain way day after day. They cultivate a certain mentality and lifestyle. Spiritual Olympians begin with habits or disciplines, think in certain trusting ways, listen to godly people, and soak up Christ regularly at private and corporate worship. They don't do this to gain God's approval or love. God's love has already been richly given. They do it in response to a desire to know the King, to be aligned with His kingdom work. They see the end result— Christlikeness—and long to be there.

Unfortunately, most of us feel the need to respond to the relentless pressure of our earthly responsibilities more often than we would like. According to the Crow study only three out of ten ministry wives found time for Bible study and prayer six or seven days in a week.[5] Predictably, these tended to be older women with no children at home. Douglas reported that thirty-eight percent of ministry wives participated in any set devotional practices that contributed to their personal or family growth. Among certain denominations, including Baptists and Evangelicals, this figure rose to fifty-five percent. Yet almost all of these women agree that they must "practice the presence of God" if they are going to gain the resources necessary for spiritual wellbeing.[6]

What does this look like? It involves resisting spiritual laziness, which brings us to that D word again—discipline. Stamina is built by exercising the muscles and resolve needed to correct the set of the sail every day as the winds of influence shift.

During a recent semester it was my privilege to gather sixteen of the world's most enjoyable people and travel to the Galapagos Islands. Our tour naturalist met us as we exited immigration. We hauled our gear onto the waiting bus and rode to the wooden dock where the gleaming sails of a yacht named the *Cachalote* shifted in the gentle swells of the Pacific. We climbed aboard for an adventure as fine as any I have had in my lifetime. The stodgy, blue-footed boobies, the black marine iguanas, the golden rays, the myriad forms that cacti can take, and the winsome ocean view from the yacht's dining area converged to entertain us for seven sparkling days.

We gathered for breakfast in the dining area of the yacht, took a dinghy to an island for a morning of hiking over uneven, always fascinating terrain, then returned to the yacht for lunch. While we ate, the yacht cut through the ocean waves to deliver us to another island of intriguing flora and fauna. It was glorious: eleven committed biology students and teachers, five interested nonscience travelers, and a crew of Spanish-speaking, charming South Americans. The mix was perfect.

Often, after a tiring day of snorkeling or hiking, we would gather on the top deck to watch the islands glide past or the dolphins race with us through the ocean. It always fascinated me that the winds that filled the sails sometimes set against us in contrary directions, yet by a slight change in the pull of the ropes, the sails sliced through the wind and directed the yacht to the exact course set by the captain, regardless of the air currents.

The moral jet streams of our society are relentlessly driving this nation's thought patterns and actions toward less moral restraint and fewer governing imperatives. It is easy to find our yacht drifting with these winds. The best way to combat the drift is to align our sail with the certainties of God's Word every day. To counter the contrary winds requires a daily adjustment of the sails of common life. This involves examining our actions in the light of scripture, shifting the ropes of our choices toward truth, what is good, and what is holy. It is ours to choose faith over cynicism. We come to know our Lord's course by lingering in His presence. We cannot know Him if we rush in scattered directions, fearing the contrary winds that keep our hearts and minds filled with the present at the expense of the hereafter.

In his book *Ordering Your Private World,* Gordon MacDonald has a number of very helpful concepts on the subject of managing one's time. If organizing your time is an issue, consider reading his very insightful book.[7]

The shortcoming of this and many other books on developing spiritual disciplines surfaces when you consider that the suggestions are often written by men who go to quiet offices and have secretaries to combat interruptions or by women who no longer have children living at home. That said, it is spiritual starvation to neglect these practices, regardless of babies, children, work, or other critical time constraints.

The Disciplines: Developing Spiritual Stamina

"Train yourself to be godly" (1 Timothy 4:7). What are these disciplines—the ones which, if practiced, keep the set of our sails aligned with a kingdom course? The following list of disciplines is adapted from those given by Gordon MacDonald.[8]

He developed spiritual exercises that he found critical to maturing in Christ.

Silence and solitude. God does not raise His voice to make himself heard above the noise of our busyness. Elijah discovered He whispers. It is very difficult to hear His voice if our heads are full of the noise of radio, conversation, active children, traffic, or the thunder of the world's industry. Silence must be nurtured and grown in our hearts if it is to exist and flourish. This is especially true in the season of life when children are young, when we are called to minister in the bustle of life with many other family members.

I love this quote from Mother Teresa:

> We need to find God, and he cannot be found in noise and restlessness. God is the friend of silence. See how nature—trees, flowers, grass—grow in silence; see the stars, the moon and sun, how they move in silence . . . the more we receive in silent prayer, the more we can give in our active life. We need silence to be able to touch souls. The essential thing is not what we say, but what God says to us and through us. All our words will be useless unless they come from within—words which do not give the light of Christ increase the darkness.[9]

Solitude—or aloneness—is difficult for many of us to pursue. It is too close a cousin to loneliness, which we avoid at all costs. Perhaps we value too much the company of others.

There is no doubt that achieving solitude involves work. "I expect that I will fight this battle of solitude and silence for as long as I live. I want to say, however, that as time has gone by, and I have begun to reap the benefits of silent time, there has been a growing hunger for more if it. But still, there is that first resistance to be overcome. When one is an activist by nature, withdrawal can be hard work. But it is necessary labor."[10]

Listen to God. Patsy Lewis is a ministry wife, author, speaker, and the leader of Potter's Clay Ministry. She developed an intriguing practice for the purpose of hearing from God. She found a quiet place and settled in with notebook and pen in hand, setting a timer for ten minutes. She simply listened to God and wrote what she believed He was saying to her. "Among other things that I wrote during that first listening time was the unexpected instruction to call the piano tuner. I obeyed, and as a result of my obedience God began giving me songs through scripture as I listened to Him."[11]

Even if you don't sense His voice, rest in the quietness of His presence. Record anything you hear from Him in a journal. These messages are a special, personal gift to you. But know that listening is hard work.

We also listen as we open God's Word and center on God's activities as recorded in Scripture. We listen as we unite our minds and ears on the minister delivering his message. It helps me focus better if I take notes on my husband's sermon so that I can bring my fingers and motor neurons into the listening process.

Keep a journal to indicate to God that what you hear from Him is worth saving on paper.

Reflection and meditation. The thing I hear from God must be internalized, not just heard. This calls for the practice of considering, then personalizing what I have heard so that it might be incorporated into my heart, my thought patterns, and my activities. MacDonald likens these two practices to pushing the "enter" key on a computer. It is the signal to execute the instruction.[12]

There are two Hebrew words used in the Bible that convey the idea of meditation. Together they are used fifty-eight times. They have meanings such as listening to God's Word, reflecting on God's works, rehearsing God's deeds, ruminating on God's laws, and more. In each case there is stress upon changed behavior as a result of our encounter with the living God.[13] Verses from Psalm 119:97, 101, 102 focus on meditation that includes obedience, a distinguishing practice of Christian meditation versus Eastern or secular meditation, which is intended to be more an enlightening experience.

What happens in meditation is that we create the emotional and spiritual space which allows Christ to construct an inner sanctuary in the heart. The wonderful verse "I stand at the door and knock . . ." was originally penned for believers . . . Meditation opens the door . . . "to Christ so that He may come in and dine with us."[14]

As I sit in my office and read these words, I understand the tendency to look hopelessly at such a project and say to myself, *I'm not sure where to even begin. Past attempts have been short-lived, basically unproductive from a human standpoint, and inadequate. How do I launch such a project?*

The desire for it is given to us as a grace gift. Believing that one can simply begin the process without praying for the desire and the grace to practice this will result in a very short-lived attempt. Having the desire and the God-instilled grace to begin heralds the promise of future grace that will encourage you to continue.[15]

Meditation also includes reflecting on God's creation. As a biologist, I love this. I have the high privilege of spending exhilarating hours learning about the creative works of God. Whether I sit before a microscope watching the photosynthetic processes of a filamentous algae, stand in a climax forest and do a line intercept study, or read an article on microarrays of cancer genes, I am overjoyed—sometimes electrified—by the wonder of God's works. There is no finer time or place to acknowledge and recognize the work of God than when studying His creation. It is pure, unmitigated fun.

How do you spend time contemplating God's majestic works? Is there a chair in your yard where you sit and watch the clouds? Is there a window you can open on a spring morning and hear the returning birds as they liven the sunrise?

Prayer. There are ways to enhance personal prayer life including praying scripture, which is turning a passage of scripture into a prayer; singing songs of praise; or speaking the lyrics of a meaningful hymn or chorus. Take a prayer walk through your home. Use pictures on a bulletin board to direct your prayers. A wonderful, white-haired saint in our first church assignment had a prayer wall of pictures she used to remember each family daily. John and I were honored when she requested a picture of us she wanted to use for that purpose.

Sometimes it seems as though the essence of our prayers rise up as vapor, dissipating in the silence of the heavens. They seem to dissolve in the sunlight or condense and fall to the earth in the cool dark of evening's end. But God has promised that they are received by Him as incense, laid with gracious hands into golden bowls where their aromas waft in His presence for eternity (Revelation 5:8). He is thus reminded of each one we repeat. None is ever lost.

Scriptural Guidance for Prayer

1 Thessalonians 5:17: We are told to pray without ceasing. Cultivate a sense that God is always at your side, listening to your thoughts. Direct your thoughts to Him.

I am such a hopeless victim of the "I can't throw this away because someday I might need it" syndrome. My closets need to feel the hands of my sister who knows how to get rid of excess stuff. Last week I stood before my bulging clothes closet and determined that once again I would get a grip on this problem. Before I began, I spoke out loud, *Jesus, you know I need you to help me clear this out. Pleeaassee, help me do the right thing.* For four hours I sorted—every drawer, every stack of sweaters, every bit of jewelry, every pair of shoes. With uncharacteristic zeal I pushed on into the afternoon. When I was tempted to dawdle over something that I have not worn in years, thinking how good it might look with my tan skirt, I prayed. The afternoon was a "prayer without ceasing" exercise. At the end I felt the joy of answered prayer and a tidy, efficient closet. Pray without ceasing. I can recommend it.

Jeremiah 33:3: When we call out to Him He has something amazing to show us. When we ask, sometimes He plants seeds of hope in us that we cannot explain. *He will give me strength, He is able to do this thing.* Amazing, isn't it!

James 4:2-3: We have to ask and do so with the right motives. Search your heart to see who will benefit most from your prayers. What is your intention? What motivates the request? Will God be glorified ultimately, or will you be more accommodated? Will your character be more improved, or will life be a little easier for you? These are not necessarily mutually exclusive, but understand your real motives.

John 16:24: When you see God answer there will be great joy. I have prayed for my children since they were conceived. John and I have travailed through tough times with each of them. We have invested countless time and incalculable hours praying for them to embrace the faith that sustains us. With credit to God's grace alone, they all serve Him and the church in their respective communities. Each time I hear my son pray or my daughters speak of their faith there is a joy that cannot be compressed into words.

Vonette Bright, cofounder of Campus Crusade for Christ, and a great advocate of prayer, gives her suggestions for enhancing your prayer life. Keep a notebook recording the dates of requests, answers to prayer, and thanksgiving.[16] This will keep your prayer time balanced and prevent it from becoming a litany of wants. It will encourage your faith in God's power to see Him answer your requests. Thanksgiving is part of what Solomon meant by "in all your ways acknowledge him" (Proverbs 3:6). As a consequence of acknowledging God, He promises to direct your paths.

These prayers need not be long or especially articulate. They can be uttered when your hands are in the dishwater or your feet are pounding out that twenty-minute workout, busy in body, but not in heart and mind. There should also be scheduled, regular moments rather than just hoped for afterthoughts, however.

Bright continues. The effort to make prayer a priority is a constant battle against the urgent. This battle is the Lord's. It is His to empower us. It is ours to be courageous. He is in this fight with us. "The purpose of prayer is to experience an intimate relationship with God in the person of Jesus Christ. The more I pray, the more I wonder why I do not pray more. The benefits are more rewarding than any other way I spend my time."[17]

Prayer should also include celebration. Celebrate what you are and what you have. Celebrate every beauty seen in the day: the privilege of working with godly people, the joy of sharing a smile with a toddler, the honest questions from a seeking heart in your Sunday School class.

As you seek to grow, keep praying to *be* more rather than *have* more. Central in my life is the tension between reaching for and holding on to what is concrete versus trusting that what I need will emerge in God's time.

I have never had a home of my own. I grew up in a parsonage, lived in rented houses for a few years, and have resided in housing owned by the church for the last forty-plus years. John and I are at a point in our lives where sometime soon we are likely to need a place of our own. For years we have talked about buying, looked at what was on the market, and discussed our dreams. In doing so, the nesting urge in me has grown in the same measure as my discontentment about living in a borrowed place.

I drive down the streets of my community, spotting all the real estate For Sale signs and ask myself, *Should we investigate that place? I wonder what it would be like to live there.* There is a growing, unsettling urgency that leaves disquiet in my days. This is my current of discontent. I have been praying that God would help me shift my focus to trust Him for my future needs. I am in need of an infusion of grace. I have been asking God to release me from the pressure of controlling this outcome at the expense of His great peace in the care of my future.

Humility. Chuck Swindoll said of humility, "It is not just a virtue; it's a discipline,"[18] a behavior to be practiced until it moves into reflexive conduct and becomes a character virtue. Pride all too often keeps us from the other disciplines. As blameless and upright as Job was, God's primary message to him in the final chapters of the book of Job seem to reveal a level of arrogance in him with which most of us can identify.

Statements I have heard: "I have read the Bible enough that I know what's in it already. I don't need to go over and over it again," or "Prayer just sometimes seems pointless," "I'm doing fine without spending so much time on practices that sometimes seem dry and uninteresting," "I have so many other priorities that there is no time for these things." These reveal a level of arrogance that suggests that we think we have arrived.

Andrew Murray, author of over 240 books, champion of the 1860 revival in South Africa, was best known for his devotional writings that emphasize the need for deep and personal spiritual life. His description of the value and importance of humility in the Christian life has stayed with me for quite some time. From his book *Humility,* he made a compelling case for this discipline. It is not something we can initiate or begin a discipline to develop. The death to self is the work of God. It is not so much a result of our own efforts, but we can discipline our thoughts and deeds to act in accordance with the grace God gives. We must be willing. The full measure of the power of this death in our disposition and conduct depends on the degree to which the Holy Spirit imparts the power of the death of Christ. This is a tough discipline for me. Like Paul in Philippians 3:12, I must admit that I have not already achieved this. Not even close. I am a work in progress, willing to be willing. I still wince at Murray's description of the practice of this discipline.

Place yourself before God in your utter helplessness. Consent heartily to the fact of your weakness to slay or make yourself alive. Sink down into your own nothingness, in the spirit of meek and patient and trustful surrender to God. Accept every humiliation, look upon every fellow-man who tries or vexes you as a means of grace to humble you. Use every opportunity of humbling yourself before your fellow-men as a help to remain humble before God. It is by the mighty strengthening of His Holy Spirit that God reveals Christ fully in you. In this manner, Christ, in His form of a servant, is truly formed in you and dwells in your heart. God will accept such humbling of yourself as the proof that your whole heart desires it. He will accept it as your very best prayer for it, and as your preparation for His mighty work of grace. It is the path of humility which leads to perfect death, the full and perfect experience that we are dead in Christ.

Then follows: *Only this death leads to perfect humility.* Oh, beware of the mistake so many make, who would like to be humble, but are afraid to be too humble. They have so many qualifications and limitations, so many reasoning and questionings, as to what true humility is to be and to do, that they never unreservedly yield themselves to it. Beware of this. Humble yourself unto the death. It is in the death to self that humility is perfected.[19]

Just to clarify, humility is neither understood nor welcomed in our society. Many government or business leaders do not view themselves as servants. They have achieved their positions by strength, sometimes cunning, often by promoting their capabilities. Not so among Christians, according to Mark 10:43-44. We are servants.

The best definition for humility that I have considered was on a poster I saw in a Sunday School class once. It announced "Humility is not thinking less of yourself. It is not thinking of yourself at all." Somehow those who practice this discipline have come to trust that the Christ of the cross can and will meet their most basic needs for love and acceptance. Thus, they are not frantically trying to convince others that they must be understood and affirmed. They are free to see the needs in others, to serve out of the overflow of grace given to and received by them in Christ.

Hope. Never give up hope. Paul, in his first letter to the Corinthians, concludes chapter 13 by listing a triplet of things that remain: faith, hope, and love; one great triune of eternal values. We see how priceless love is. Faith is the essential offering that brings us into relationship with God. Much less often do I hear the value of *hope*. Yet it ranks right up there. Keep hoping no matter what. God is intent on growing you in Him. He will be faithful. We, of all people, Christians imbued with promises from the Maker of all things, should remain hopeful about God's love, His plan in our lives, the future, the church, our family.

There is a wearisome perfusion of hopelessness in the conversations that revolve around what some see as the appalling condition of the world today. They range from who is or isn't in the White House, the state of the economy, the inability to find a job commensurate with one's education, the state of global warming, the uncertainties of the health care system, the conditions of the public school system and disrespectful children, poverty, and HIV/AIDS in third world countries and on and on and on. It is tempting to embrace the murky pessimism that clouds the voices of those without hope.

Here is a list of verses to encourage you to put your hope in God and His loving kindness: Psalm 31:24; 33:18; 39:7; 43:5; 119:74; Romans 5:3-5.

It may be easy to get discouraged after reading a chapter filled with descriptions of Christian disciplines that appear so out of our reach that we are filled with guilt over our failure to achieve them. There is no subject that induces more guilt than these. Rather than berating yourself over your lack, try to remember that God is always willing to meet you where you are and move you slowly into His deeper graces. Be willing to try. Pray and ask Him to give you the desire and the grace to begin. Know that this work may illustrate the three-steps-forward-two-steps-backward principle, but God is greater than your hesitation, stronger than your hopeless resignation. Reach out and let Him gently pull you along. Christian maturity is the greatest weapon we have in experiencing the joy of ministry.

But what if you have tried and the praying, the reading of God's Word, and the trusting no longer bring you near to God? In fact, what if it only makes life worse; you feel even more guilt? What if life in the ministry is so distressing that you no longer find peace in any of these acts of faith? Come, let's look together at what the darkness of this place looks like, who you share this spot with, and what is the perspective of other women who have come and left this place of great discouragement.

First, though, let's look at the common, garden variety of discouragement, its causes, and the strategies women suggest for overcoming it.

■ FOR YOUR CONSIDERATION

1. What do you think is the biggest stumbling block that inhibits most ministry wives from exercising these disciplines?
2. Have you overcome this or some other stumbling block in your spiritual maturing? How?
3. What part of the natural world inspires you to thank God?
4. What do you struggle with regarding the disciplines in this chapter?
5. How is your prayer life contributing to your ministry?

Meditate on these and consider what they say. James 4:8a; Proverbs 8:17; John 16:13; John 8:31b-32.

NINE

Advice for the Discouraged

The truth is that our finest moments are most likely to occur when we are feeling deeply uncomfortable, unhappy, or unfulfilled. For it is only in such moments, propelled by our discomfort, that we are likely to step out of our ruts and start searching for different ways or truer answers. (**Scott Peck**)

In my research I have heard scores of stories from women who have detailed their frustrations. I have distilled the responses of the women in my own survey as well as six other surveys, plus the words of a dozen or so authors whose writing and experience I have come to value. What follows in this chapter is a digest of their advice on how to manage issues four through fourteen of the top fourteen things that seem to discourage ministry wives. These are not *the* most pressing concerns but are worth addressing.

The Good and the Bad of the Other Problems

Besides my own expectations, the unrealistic expectations of others, loneliness, and my husband's schedule (the top four), ministry wives are frustrated by, in no particular order, feelings of failure, guilt, and resentment; helplessness in the face of troubling situations; overcommitment; goldfish bowl living; church politics and problems; people in the church who refuse to seek God or spiritual maturity; and inadequate finances.

What goes wrong when I give in to feelings such as false guilt? For one thing, it keeps me from responding with a gracious but firm *no* to some requests. When I say *yes* to avoid the guilt of saying no, I suffer something far worse: the knowledge that I have taken on responsibility that belongs to someone else whom God is calling to do the task and equipping for that work. For this reason, guilt makes the pace of my life insane at times.

Many struggle with feelings of failure. This is how that looks in the life of a ministry wife. One fall evening my good friend and I waited in the fellowship hall of the church for the great host of people we were expecting for a women's night out. We had chosen a well-qualified speaker, printed and distributed five hundred door hangers for our church neighborhood homes, arranged for great snacks, announced it in the church bulletin and in the services, recruited women to be greeters, servers, and cleaners, and we stood at the door waiting for the eager faces to materialize. The disappointment was palpable when the only ones who showed up were the women recruited to do the jobs assigned. That evening a hopeful, little blue thread broke in the tapestry of my ministry, and the space that it left unfinished took months, if not years, to rethread.

Is there anything good about struggling with these painful issues? It's interesting that twenty-three percent of the women in my survey indicate they very rarely get discouraged about being in ministry. This is both delightful and poignant. Those of us who have had difficulties report that it is the strain of the adjustment that provides the momentum for growth toward a more powerful service and the motivation for introspection. Effective ministry is sometimes done best by "wounded healers."

Things to Keep in Mind

There are a few principles that should be understood before you consider the collective sage advice of all these ministry wives. There are stages of ministry, and the following advice is likely to be more helpful to those who are in an early stage. The overwhelming majority of women who endure the challenges of being a ministry wife report that the growth and struggle were worth it.

Also, this advice will probably be most helpful to women who find ministry very challenging. According to Douglas, these are women who tend to be more analytical, sensitive, reflective, talented, educated, introverted, and reserved.[1]

Second, the most fulfilled ministry wives carry as their mantra the commitment to care rather than self-fulfillment. It's an interesting and ancient paradox that we are least likely to find fulfillment when we put its pursuit at the head of our priorities. It comes as a byproduct rather than a product. That has a biblical ring; something about seeking God's kingdom—and His priority to love others—first, then what we need and find fulfilling come as a byproduct. It appears that most ministry wives understand this on some level, but the practice of this caring priority is a challenge for many who are tempted to believe their own desires and fulfillment are top priority. Giving up self-interests can be tough.

Third, fulfillment is also associated with maintaining a sense of humor, and as Douglas puts it, "Ride easy in the saddle."[2] I have heard this advice from many quarters. Learn to laugh and view yourself through the colorful lens of humor.

Fulfillment involves learning to speak the truth in love without taking oneself and one's limited understanding of the situation too seriously.

I have been teaching so long that I have engraved on the frontal lobe of my brain all the problems associated with communicating accurately to people—in my case often students— and clearly understanding the situation as it is. No matter how lucid the state of affairs appears to you, there is something you are not seeing. Take your own opinion with a grain of salt. Lighten up. "It means combining a sense of ultimacy with a light touch, work with love, play, and worship."[3]

Fourth, on a more outward perspective, it helps to remember that the church is filled neither with the culture of the perfected nor with the saints arrived, but with the imperfect in progress. As a hospital is to the wounded and sick, so is the church to the spiritually needy. It is the sick who need a doctor, as Jesus pointed out. Somehow, we are too often surprised by sickness in the church.

Fifth, from the perspective of the family, frustration and discouragement are regularly magnified when there are children at home. In Crow's research, wives who have children at home express significantly more often a need for help with feelings of guilt, lack of self-confidence, discouragement, and managing emotions than those wives without children at home.[4] Remember: this too will pass. Interestingly, you are less likely to express a need for help in one or more of the above areas if you are over forty, are in a longer tenure at a church, have a church of over one hundred in attendance, and have a job.[5] This last point is open to some debate. Working outside the home can be both a blessing and a burden. For me, it was a great blessing, even though it was very draining.

Advice from Other Ministry Wives

From the heaps of helpful ideas offered by and for ministry wives, I distilled them into three advice categories:

- Managing your perspective of yourself
- Managing your perspective of your family
- Managing your service to the church

MANAGING YOUR PERSPECTIVE OF YOURSELF

When ministry wives in my survey are asked what helps them most, what carries them through difficult times, the number one answer was related to some aspect of spiritual maturity: Bible reading, prayer, meditation. This figure is even higher in the survey of Hsieh and Rugg.[6]

After advice on developing your spiritual life, the most common recommendation for managing discouragement or having a healthy attitude on ministry in the survey I conducted and in several others was to *focus on the positive*. Statements such as "count your blessings," "gain a long-term perspective," "create a new hope for the future," "believe this too shall pass" were commonly expressed.

I was reminded of the value of focusing on the positive during a recent visit to Japan. I was traveling with a group of students and faculty, and we visited the Tofu House in Kyoto. We were invited to enjoy sesame tofu with a small froth of wasabi, grilled tofu with sweet miso, miso soup, egg custard with eel, and ginkgo nut. The foods of Japan are so unfamiliar to my palate that following the dinner there, I felt the need to express my thoughts on the subject to a compatriot traveling with me.

The evening was sharply colored by an accidental ingestion of the entire tuft of green wasabi, which felt like flame in my mouth that traveled with piercing intensity down my esophagus. I decided I had had enough Japanese food for a while.

My complaints to my friend were met with a statement that gave me such pause that I will remember it as a turning point in my outlook on the trip. She said, "The overall evening at the restaurant was so magnificent that I would like to remember the experience as wonderfully positive, even though there were parts of it that I did not like."

In other words, quit complaining and savor the privileges of the evening. I stood rightly rebuked, and I have come to cherish her counsel. Can you imagine being in arguably the most scenic city of Japan and in the best tofu restaurant there and focusing on the part of the whole evening that was less than ideal? Suggestion: Refocus on the positive.

Ministry is like that. There will be days when, out of all the things that happen to you, one powerful frustration will stick in your throat. If you let it, it will spoil the beauty of the day. The sour comments of a senior citizen in response to a change in the ministry style will blind you to the blessing of the smile on a child's face when you tousle his hair. A disagreement in a committee meeting can obscure an entire week of simple joys in sharing in the loving acts of the congregation. Proverbs 15:15 indicates, "The cheerful heart has a continual feast." Japanese or otherwise.

Positive thinking is not denial of the disturbing events or "moths" that fly around your little light. It is stopping to evaluate the moths and discovering they are mostly things you have no control over—or that they will pass or are not your responsibility—then choosing to center on cherishing the light.

From many sources it is recommended to *know, care for, and develop yourself*—not to the exclusion of serving others, but to be a steward of God's gifts to you. Know your strengths, your spiritual gifts, your areas of weakness, or as business companies call them, "developmental opportunities." Know how God sees and affirms you. If you have not taken a spiritual gifts test, find one online and take it. Then, develop your gifts. Attend workshops to help you deepen these abilities. Most colleges allow people to audit courses rather inexpensively. Take advantages of this. Work from your strengths. If you have gifts in the area of teaching but not in administration, agree to teach the first grade class rather than manage the children's department. I find working with small children an area in which I am not gifted, so I handle registration and some aspects of the finance in Vacation Bible School.

What if no one else takes the leadership role and you are not gifted in administration? Is there someone in the church who has latent skills in this area that can be encouraged to develop them? Go with her to a workshop on how to do VBS, or take her for a chat with a woman in your area who has done VBS and can give advice and support. Work as a coleader with her to encourage the development of her skills.

Try not to work from your weaknesses; it is a recipe for frustration. Learn to graciously but firmly decline without guilt. When asked to take a job, prayerfully consider whether or not you are equipped to step in. "That looks like a great project, I am so glad you have taken some responsibility for the work, but I understand my strengths and weaknesses, and this area is one in which I have no skills or aptitude. Let's see if we can come up with a few names of people who work well here."

Forget trying to be a superwoman; that will take the joy out of ministry. Pat Valeriano suggests that when your husband interviews for a church and you are asked about your role there, graciously review your strengths with the board and suggest that as God leads you will be happy to serve in these areas.[7]

Recognize and maintain your individuality with humility and grace. Recognize your distinctiveness so that you may not be deflected by how someone else you admire may be doing the job or by how someone else thinks you should do it. You can gain from them, but in so doing merely polish who you are.

Recognize how your set of gifts, motivations, and temperament will or won't work in each situation. I remember as a young person hearing Ann Kimmel, a charismatic woman of God, and deciding that I wanted to be just like her. In reality, she has influenced my development, but I have managed to avoid the exasperating trap of really trying to be just like her.

Care for yourself, spiritually, physically, mentally, and emotionally. Become a person of quality and depth, not because you are the pastor's wife, but because God has called you to do whatever you do as unto the Lord—with excellence. It means eating healthy, exercising, taking care to look as good as you can on the budget you have.

I remember fifteen years ago being motivated to dismiss the excuse that I had no time for exercise. In addition to seeing the poor results of a bone scan, I remember reading a story in Stephen Covey's book *7 Habits of Highly Effective People* that goes something like this.

Once in the green and full forests of the north, a young, strong man decided that he would cast his lot among the lumberjacks of that North Country. He traveled along the logging roads one brilliant afternoon in search of the foreman of the lumbering company in which he was interested. At the end of the gravel path he sighted a small log cabin office with a sign above the door that indicated he had arrived at the local office of the company. He knocked on the door and was greeted by a cheerful, stocky man in a red flannel shirt.

"Are you the foreman of this lumber company?" he inquired.

"Yes," replied the stocky man in the red flannel shirt.

The young man set out his thoughts to the foreman and applied for a position. Eager to have this strong young man join the company, the foreman gave him an axe and some advice.

"In the first week or so you will probably cut down three trees a day. Don't be discouraged, you will develop the skills and strength to cut four the second week and maybe five by next month. Work hard and if you become really good at this, you may eventually cut six trees in a day. Very few men do this, but you are young and strong. I think you may have what it takes."

Early the next morning as the sun rose to heat the day, the young man accompanied the lumberjacks into the pine forest to begin his work. True to the foreman's words, he cut down three trees with help from the other men of the group. By the end of the week, he could manage three trees on his own. By the end of the second week he was delivering four trees to the transport truck parked at the entrance of the clearing. As he began his third week he was astonished to discover he could only manage to fell three trees a day. Frustrated, he worked harder, swinging his axe with exaggerated fury. In the middle of the week the foreman dropped by to check on his young protégé and discovered the concerns of the young man.

"Have you stopped to sharpen your axe?" inquired the foreman after a moment's thought.

The young man responded as he continued to rain forceful blows upon the tree, "No, I don't have time."[8]

That story stopped me in my tracks. The seventh habit of highly effective people is "sharpen the saw." I have come to understand that when I take the time to take care of myself, exercise properly, make time to put together healthful meals, I can get more done, feel better, sleep better, and be more temperamentally good-natured. I find that a good workout releases a wad of pent-up, adrenalinized aggravation.

A word of caution: If you find that you are going under emotionally, get outside help. The fees for professional counseling in our area are calculated on a sliding scale, so some therapists can be very reasonably priced. In my survey, eighty-one percent of the women who have experienced dysthymia or depression and have gone for professional counseling have found this "definitely helpful." Another fifteen percent found it "somewhat helpful." Only four percent said it was not helpful. I see a resounding endorsement for professional help when you need it!

Roy Oswald gives six suggestions for avoiding clergy wife burnout. Among them he indicates you need to find appropriate pastoral support, preferably not your husband. Is there a local, more experienced female minister or associate pastor who can listen to and pray with you? Develop a support network that can stand with you.

Try to connect with other ministry wives of somewhat like mind in your area. If you try to connect with someone who is delighted with all that ministry provides, and you are entirely frustrated with the situation, it may prove to be a less than ideal relationship. Likewise, be equally careful about connecting with someone who is very disillusioned about ministry. This could turn into a situation of the blind leading the blind.

Oswald even suggests that some ministry wives could benefit from assertiveness training so they might learn to be graciously firm about their needs. This is not training that results in belligerence, mean-spiritedness, or self-centeredness, but rather training that improves the communication skills of reticent ministry wives.[9]

Taking care of yourself means taking some time to be off-task. If you need an excuse or you feel guilty about taking a break, remember that even God had a Sabbath. Repeatedly, women give the advice to take time off. Short on funds? Go to the library and sit on a comfortable chair for an hour or two and read a book or a magazine, or just sit quietly while your husband stays with the kids. Take a walk in the park with your dog or another woman who needs a break. Again, if God needed a day of rest, so do you.

Ruth Senter, in her wonderful little book *The Guilt-Free Book for Pastors' Wives,* has a chapter on how to manage your feelings and emotions. This is an area some pastors' wives should address to help make life in ministry more enjoyable for them. Senter's solutions? Acknowledge and express your feelings at an appropriate place and time. When possible, anticipate your feelings. If you know your husband will be away for a retreat and you are likely to experience loneliness, plan a night out with a girlfriend or go visit your sister, kids and all.[10]

As much as possible, control the negative aspects of your emotions. You have been given the spirit of self-control, according to Galatians 5:22-23. Self-control helps keep things in perspective. According to 2 Peter 1:8, if you keep developing this quality and others listed in the previous verses, they will keep you from being ineffective and unproductive in your knowledge of Christ.

Although I still work on managing these feelings, here is something I have learned. For several years I delivered five or six lectures per semester to students studying criminal justice in a forensic science course. One of the lectures was on the importance and practice of autopsies.

During that class I used clips from an actual autopsy to illustrate points in the lecture, and students were always fascinated by the process—if they could tolerate the pictures. Fortunately, most could. I explained the purpose of an autopsy was to determine the cause of death. Often the information from such procedures is used as data in studies of certain diseases.

The experience of a failure resulting in feelings of inadequacy deserves a good autopsy. The failure needs to be held out and looked at carefully to determine the cause and the prevention of a future occurrence. These kinds of autopsies are very helpful. Here's where it goes awry: some of us can get our emotions pulled down into the corpse of the failure and get stuck feeling as if *we* are the failure. Then the work of the autopsy is deferred, and no good comes of the whole thing. The dissecting table of a failure is no place to get stuck emotionally. Step back from the corpse and keep your emotional distance as you evaluate how to implement future corrections. Let it be your teacher, not your bully.

MANAGING YOUR PERSPECTIVE OF YOUR FAMILY

I found a wagonload of advice in all the surveys about how to manage your perspective on the family, and almost uniformly they declare your family should come first. Your first duty on earth is to husband and family. Arrive at a balance between your responsibility to others and to your family. Zoba lists three key factors necessary for health and wholeness in ministry wives, one of which is a solid relationship with one's husband.[11] London and Wiseman even put out a Bill of Rights for ministry wives that includes advice on helping your husband and maintaining a close relationship with him.[12]

Most of us understand on a philosophical level that our families take priority, but the boundaries that maintain that practice are sometimes nebulous and are exposed to so much pressure they often give way or become obscured by the surprises of each day. Here's a little different way of thinking about priorities.

All the relatives I knew growing up lived in Kansas, and a trip to Kansas was as exciting to me then as a trip to another continent is to me now. I loved being at my cousins' homes. They lived on farms and had acres of play area and scores of novel amusements, which I adored.

My uncle had a device perched on the cabinet in his dining room that I have come to understand is called a Galileo Thermometer. It was a slender, glass cylindrical apparatus filled with a fluid in which drifted ten colorful floating glass bubbles with metal tags hanging below each. The tags had numbers stamped on them that corresponded to temperatures. In order to determine the ambient room temperature, I read the number on the tag of the highest—or lowest, I can't remember which—floating bubble. The bubbles would cheerfully rise and sink as the temperature changed. I was fascinated and spent many wonder-filled moments watching the rise and fall of the green, red, and yellow bubbles.

Priorities are like that. In the fluidity of my days I found that sometimes I had to attend to driving my youngest to a music lesson. It was the most important thing at that moment. I chatted with her and encouraged the musician inside her. Sometimes I got my oldest daughter to drive her, and I could take care of a parishioner on the phone. That was more important at that moment. Sometimes a music concert took priority over Wednesday night prayer meeting; sometimes the prayer meeting took priority over my son's need for help with a homework assignment. I could help him after the meeting. True, my son has a higher priority than the church, but help with his homework assignment from seven to eight on Wednesday night does not have priority over prayer with the women of my church from seven to eight. Although there was flexibility, my family priorities rose to the top more often than not.

Most often rising to the top of your family priorities should be your relationship with your husband. Six of the twenty components in the Bill of Rights for the ministry wife include advice on your relationship with your husband.[13] This advice is reiterated in many of the resources used in this book.

Twenty-three percent of the written responses to the question "What helps you when you are discouraged/dysthymic/depressed?" in my survey included some reference to "my husband." The health of that connection cannot be overstated. Spend quality time with him. Make your home a refuge for him. Work to develop a healthy communication system so that the lines between your lives are clear and strong. There are a great many books on this subject as well as ample marriage seminars and workshops. It is worth the effort to develop a close bond with your husband.

MANAGING YOUR SERVICE TO THE CHURCH

What should your attitude be toward your congregation? From all quarters comes the resounding response: love them, cultivate a focus on caring. This is more difficult for some of us than for others. We are task-driven Marthas, and our culture does us no great favor by pressing us to stand and deliver as our number one priority. This does not mean that we abandon a quality effort to chat on the phone with a friend. It has more to do with the rise and fall of the glass bubbles in the thermometer. These two things, caring for your congregation and working at a task with excellence, are not mutually exclusive, but they can bump into each other inconveniently. The suggestion is that the caring part of your work should rise to the top more often.

It's a sometimes puzzling, confusing thing to figure out what *love them* means. I do not throw out this mandate lightly. For some, like my mother, love continually rolls from their hearts as naturally as water splashes over the stones of a waterfall. But for all of us love is a lifetime pursuit. We work at it until the day we cross the finish line and leave all earthly congregations behind. We pray for God to love according to His priorities, and we ask God to turn what sometimes feels like duty into delight.

As much as is possible, be a woman of hospitality.

On a more practical side, here are some bits of wisdom paraphrased from the Bill of Rights for Pastors' Wives by London and Wiseman.

- Don't attempt to control the church by giving advice and then becoming annoyed because it isn't followed.
- Listen more and talk less.
- Nurture women in your congregation who will make a difference in the church and the world. These are change agents.

- Show visible love to your husband in the presence of the church. Hold hands in the foyer.
- Don't spiritualize everything to the congregation. Some things that happen are not God's will. Don't blame Him. Doing so may sound like a dismissal of someone's pain.
- Be yourself, but don't be bizarre or eccentric. Be a woman of decency and propriety (1 Timothy 2:9).
- Be a keen and accurate observer of the church. Let your husband know your impression of the situation by such charming comments as "Have you considered this perspective?" "Does this make sense to you?"
- Ask God to help you see the people in your church the way He sees them.[14]

Hear this wisdom from Mother Teresa: "Keep giving Jesus to your people not by words—but by your example, by your being in love with Jesus—by radiating His holiness and spreading His fragrance of love everywhere you go. Just keep the joy of Jesus as your strength—be happy and at peace, accept whatever He gives—and give whatever He takes with a big smile."

■ FOR YOUR CONSIDERATION

1. Finish this statement: "When it comes to handling my emotions I feel that I am . . ."
2. How does one make one's home a haven in the face of the needs of the congregation?
3. If you have nurtured or mentored women in your church, what have you learned in the process?
4. What feelings do you struggle with that seem to be detrimental to your joy?

TEN

When Ministry Gets Tough

God whispers to us in our pleasures, speaks to us in our conscience, but shouts in our pains: It is His megaphone to rouse a deaf world. (C. S. Lewis)

I started down what eventually became the road to this book as a direct result of the depression experience of a pastor's wife who committed suicide. At the time I could see only the near horizon of my own life, and in those skies it was written in bold letters: "Somebody needs to help us." I had no plan to be of help, only a strong conviction that someone, somewhere needed to help women like Jenna before they considered ending their lives.

As each new arc of my horizon rolled forward, I could see a next step to take, and after many steps and many years I have come to this chapter in this book. Most of the previous chapters have been about dealing with the normal—though often overwhelming—pressures of ministry. I have always had in mind the twenty-two percent of ministry wives who report they have experienced depression. Another twelve percent have endured dysthymia.

It is the purpose of this chapter to shed some light on this subject, but more importantly to give hope to those in the crush of this darkness. Women who have gone through this need information, but more than that they need hope that God is at work, that He has some personal interest in their travails, that there is an unexplained plan to make them more valuable to His kingdom work. They need to see some purpose in this thing. Hanging on to this hope—this thin, bright thread—is what may carry them to the dawn where joy comes in brilliance.

What Depression and Dysthymia Look Like

A few years back Lynn Hybels, ministry wife of Bill Hybels who pastors the megachurch Willow Creek Community Church, came to speak in chapel at the school where I teach. Her honest, open reflections on her own experience of depression were poignant and riveting. I was so captivated by what she said that I purchased her intriguing book, *Nice Girls Don't Change the World*. In it she describes her experience, which involved the decision to walk away from God.

Hybels' childhood construct of God would not allow her soul to experience peace. He was demanding, required unreasonable striving, and allowed no time of soul quiet, which she desperately needed. She was unable to manage the possibility that life would continue to be governed by more of this same God. She understood that the only way to find the rest she longed for was to abandon the God of her childhood, a frightening thought indeed. So on a hot summer day, stretched out on the deck of a sailboat, she looked up into the clouds and ventured this conversation.

I can't do it anymore, I said. *I can't keep striving for your love. Maybe there is a God somewhere who doesn't drain the life out of people, but I don't know who that God is. You're the only God I know, and I can't carry the burden of you anymore.*

She did not broadcast her decision. She was just done with what she perceived as a God who sucked the life out of her.

As she views this series of events in retrospect, she understands that the true God of grace and love had actually set her free from the childhood construct of God that she had been serving. Even in her depression, she understood that she would not have released this construct of God had she not heard the whisper of the Spirit of a different God say, *I know your soul needs healing from the wounds of this false god. So go ahead, turn your back and walk away. You will be OK.*

So I dropped the burden of my childhood God and I rested. There were still tasks and duties I simply had to muster the energy to attend to. But whenever possible, I did the only thing I truly had energy for: I sat in an easy chair and looked out the window.

She sat in the chair and watched the summer leaves turn golden and red, the winter snows pile up on the Illinois grasses, the birds sing spring songs in the crabapple tree. She yielded to the beauties of nature. She listened to music, and in the quiet of her private days she began to dance, enjoying tiny sparkling bits of life's pleasures.

After a time her soul began to respond to the mind rest and soul freedom, and she noticed a longing for God again; a new kind of God. She opened her heart, "just a crack, to this mysterious Presence, knowing that if I heard even one syllable of the demanding rhetoric of my childhood God, I could immediately slam shut the door to my heart—and I was fully prepared to do that."

She decided to risk an approach, to speak softly into the darkness two little words, "It's me." And God's astounding answer was a love-engendered embrace that even now she views as the pivotal moment of her life. To be embraced by the true God of the cross changes everything.[1]

Sue Monk Kidd, *New York Times* best-selling author of the *Secret Life of Bees*, experienced just such a pivotal moment also. Her encounter began during the Christmas season.

In the middle of the busyness of holiday decorating she stood at the top of a ladder working to put the Christmas tree right when she was struck suddenly with chest pains. Her doctor declared the pains were stress related and ordered her to rest. In the stillness of that rest she sat, silent, reflecting on her life. The familiar ache of emptiness, the obscure longing for an unnamed something rose above her previous intensive efforts to obscure them. In desperation she read the Bible and came upon the story of the angel that troubled the waters at the pool of Bethesda.

"I had been lying on the porticoes of my life for years. Now I had come upon a 'certain season,' some holy moment when I must wade into the empty hunger that swirled beneath the surface of my life. I knew there would be no wholeness unless I stepped down into my darkness and confronted the troubling angel within."[2]

For weeks she sat in an agony of stillness, reflecting, praying, retreating, as she confronted the troubling angel. It was that same false God of her childhood that Lynn Hybels faced: the one that drove her toward perfectionist behaviors and relentless striving. Surviving on little blue tranquilizers, she gazed beneath the surface of her broken life and realized that she was starving for the immediacy of a loving God. The understanding of this need and the image of the troubling angel marked the beginning of her journey outward and into the fierce tenderness of God's love.

Through solitude and silence I began to find an inner music, a love song being sung in the spaces of my own heart. In the mystery of contemplative prayer I learned to enter God's presence within and experience myself being loved beyond reason. . . . The pain I experienced on the ladder at Christmas became the sacred hinge of my life, a pivotal experience.[3]

As I reflect on my own experience with dysthymia, a more persistent but less severe form of depression, I am convinced it was more situational than anything else. The converging currents of my life brought my soul into a vortex of doubt about the God of my childhood. God worked in the same way, said some of the same things, and brought me into the same warm daylight these two women felt.

If you are feeling the surging currents of doubt, the black depths of hopelessness, the clear understanding that the demanding God of your childhood is not working, read on. There is a different God who longs to show you His love if only you will release the other one, the one you are now clinging to.

How It Happens

Psychologists distinguish several kinds of depression with different causes: major depression—severe, lasting about two weeks; dysthymic disorder—milder, but lasting longer; manic depression—cyclic; postpartum depression—after the birth of a baby, affects ten to twenty percent of new mothers; seasonal affective disorder—occurring at a particular time of the year; anxiety depression; atypical depression; chronic depression; double depression—dysthymia and depression together; endogenous depression—no outward apparent reason; situational depression—occurs in response to stressful situations; agitated depression; psychotic depression; and catatonic depression.[4]

Common causes include loss, transition, medical conditions, physical changes in the body, personality traits, stresses, unresolved anger, unrepentant sin or rebellion, occult involvement, negative thinking, medications, diet, alcohol and drug intoxication and withdrawal, neurodegenerative diseases, viral infections.[5]

About one-third of depressive episodes have biochemical roots and respond to medication. In my survey, of the eighty-one ministry wives who admitted to episodes of either dysthymia or depression and who were taking prescription medication, sixty-nine (eighty-five percent) said the medication was helpful. Fifteen reported medication did not help. Keep in mind that most medication takes time to work, and the time frame that recurs repeatedly in the literature is about six weeks. Here are symptoms that can indicate biochemical depression:

- You have been depressed for a long time despite changes in your life.
- Talk therapy has little or no effect; in fact, psychological probing questions such as "Why do you hate your father?" leave you as confused as Alice at the Mad Hatter's tea party.
- You don't react to good news.
- You awaken very early in the morning and can't get back to sleep.
- You cannot trace the onset of your depression to any event in your life.
- Your mood may swing between depression and elation over a period of months in a regular rhythm (this suggests bipolar or manic-depressive disorder).

- Drinking alcohol worsens your depression the following day.[6]

Some episodes of depression respond to counseling therapy without medication. Of the seventy women who engaged in counseling, sixty-six reported that it was either "definitely helpful," or "somewhat helpful." If you are besieged by depressive or dysthymic episodes, seriously consider counseling or discussing this with your family physician. For most of the women in my survey, this was the help they needed.

The women in my survey who identified their experience as depression or dysthymia recognized that there were surrounding circumstances that contributed to their suffering. Half of them suggested that reproductive issues—pregnancy, postpartum, or menopause—framed their experience. About one-third saw the demands of small children as a contributing element. High on the list of contributing factors was church and financial problems. One term for the type of suffering that originates from stressful events is "situational depression."

It begins when negative thinking spreads to negative feelings, then to negative perceptions of the world or the future. According to Linda Mintle, writer, speaker, and professor at Wheaton College, most depression begins with negative thinking. "I am hopeless." "No one cares about me." "The world will be better off if I disappear." Help lies in breaking these negative thought patterns.[7]

In the next chapter you will read the stories of three ministry wives. One required medication to break the cycle of depressive thoughts; one required counseling; and one found her way back to wholeness with the help of neither of these two. You may identify with one of these three solutions, but whichever you see as a potential help, take the steps necessary to begin the process.

Depression often affects your view of God, who seems far away, indifferent, or incapable. Part of the work of healing is restoring your belief in God; and in my experience He is very willing to help you with this.

Some depressions seem to have a genetic component. Forty-six percent or roughly half of the women in my survey who experienced dysthymia or depression affirmed a family history.

There are many great books, articles, seminars, and Web sites that discuss this in depth and give story after story about recovery from this gripping darkness. If you need information, these resources, presented by qualified Christian men and women, can be of great value to you. Here are just a few that I found informative, readable, and encouraging.

- "Escaping the Swamp of Depression," an article by Pastor David Currie gives insight into how a pastor and his supportive wife got to the other side.[8]

- *Breaking Free from Depression: A Balanced Biblical Strategy for Emotional Freedom,* by Linda Mintle, a book that describes those who get depressed, why it happens, and what the biblical principles for recovery look like. It's short and very readable.[9]

- *Seven Things That Steal Your Joy,* by Joyce Meyer, describes factors that contribute to and bring relief from discouragement.[10]

- *Unveiling Depression in Women: A Practical Guide to Understanding Depression,* by Archibald Hart and his daughter Catherine Hart Weber, gives in-depth information about causes and strategies for help, health, and healing.[11]

What Seems to Help

The cause of the depression will determine what treatment will be helpful. There are many underlying biological causes such as hypoglycemia, vitamin deficiency, menopause, and postpartum hormonal adjustments, to name a few. The first step is to have a thorough physical checkup and overall health evaluation. Relief may be as simple as vitamins or changing your diet.

If stressful circumstances seem to trigger depression, the solution may include altering the stressful pressures as much as you can. Work it out with your husband or other moms to watch your children a couple of hours every week to give you a chance to do something you enjoy that will help relieve your stress. I used my time alone to visit the local library to read magazines, check out my favorite author, peruse the *New York Times,* or listen to wonderful music. Since I had very little discretionary funds and this was free, I felt no guilt.

Go for a walk in the park with a friend. Go to a seminar or read a great book.

There is a physical component to the battle with depression. A good workout can drain away a large chunk of stress. This is confirmed by a small but significant number of women in my survey.

Two-thirds of the affected women in my survey indicated they received help from practicing some aspect of the spiritual disciplines—listening to inspiring music or reading Scripture and encouraging books. Not everyone finds these things helpful, however. If you find that in spite of your efforts to connect with God, you still feel as Lynn Hybels and I did—that He is as distant as the midnight stars—know that He is still collecting your prayers in His golden dish.

Don't give up on God. You may have to release your child-hood God, but don't close your heart on an eternal, loving God. Give Him just a bit of faith, a little crack in the door, a little bargaining room. Hebrews 11:6 tell us that without faith it is impossible to please God, because anyone who comes to Him must believe that He exists and that He rewards those who earnestly seek Him.

Verbalize the promises of God. Even if you don't feel like it, make yourself do it. Isaiah 61:2-3, 2 Corinthians 12:9-10, and the Psalms are places to look, read, and read again.

If the causes of your depression can be identified and you have some control over them, take charge. Recognize and deal with repressed anger, work to resolve family conflicts, recognize and relieve inappropriate guilt or shame, and forgive those who have hurt you.

If you find yourself beset by episodes of discouragement about the stressful events in your life, be of good cheer, you are in good company. Joseph, Moses, Elijah, Ezra, Nehemiah, Job, Solomon, Jesus, John the Baptist, Paul, and Peter were all under the spell of disillusionment or discouragement at some point in their ministry.

If medication is needed, don't hesitate to use it. Sarah Baldauf cites the groundbreaking 2006 STAR*D trial that suggests that "one-third of people found total relief with their first drug and about one-third were not helped even after trying several drugs and combinations." This same trial also showed that cognitive behavioral therapy (CBT) after the unsuccessful first medication works about as well as a second medication. This therapy focuses on correcting destructive thought patterns; something like "renewing your mind" that the writer of the book of Hebrews talks about.[12]

Both counseling and medication are options if they are indicated. God and medicine are not mutually exclusive. If you and your physician have found that you need medicine, you haven't let God down. Use what you need.

Three Christian Perspectives on Learning from Depression

Over the past decade or two I have paid particular attention to what is said by Christian people who have experienced depression. Their insights and experiences have spoken to me, and their words linger and surface in my quiet contemplations. These ruminations have brought a sigh of relief to something that is just beyond the reach of my explanation. Let me share their comments with you. I am praying that they will speak to you in that same way.

During a recent fall semester, I attended the class of Dr. Richard Middleton, professor of Old Testament, on the Wisdom Literature. His discussion on Psalms intrigued me. He suggested that the Psalms can be grouped into three general types, some of which overlap and contain elements of each of these types. These groups include the *poems of orientation,* which represent the feelings and thoughts of those who are experiencing a season of well-being—of joyfulness so that praise to God is natural and spontaneous. The second type includes those he called *poems of disorientation* where life consists of hurt, alienation, suffering, and death and evoke feelings common to those in depression: lament, hyperbole, resentment, self-pity, and hatred. The third group of psalms are those of *reorientation or new orientation,* which reflect the joys and relief of recovery from the darkness.

He considers these three types of poems representative of the lives of many believers. The new believer experiences a useful but somewhat immature perception of God and can rejoice in this view. At some point it becomes necessary to develop a more mature reading of God and faith, and this new insight requires a painful surrender of the old way of thinking; hence, the disorientation. Finally, as this progression is successful, a new and more valued picture of God emerges, one that will sustain a new position in life.[13]

Dr. Middleton wove into this lecture his personal experience of depression that began with great disillusionment and led him to a new level of commitment to Christ. I was struck by this biblical picture of his depression and what I perceived in my life as a time devoid of spiritual meaning. It is the story much like the life, death, and resurrection of Christ.

Author, educator, and activist Parker Palmer came to speak at our campus several years ago and ignited in me an interest in his ideas. This tall, stately man has suffered through multiple bouts of clinical depression. During one session with his therapist, he was drawn to a new perception of this period in his life.

Parker's therapist said to him, "Parker, you look at depression as an enemy that is intent on crushing you. Can you consider that depression is a friend trying to hold you down to ground where it is safe to walk?" His insightful therapist was pointing out to Palmer that the self-expectations and perceptions of God and faith that were incubating in his heart were not those that could sustain him. This dark period in his life had purpose; to allow a new and more relational perception of God to rise from the ashes of his blackness and allow him to walk on more stable ground.[14]

Joyce Meyer has some advice on how to use your very distasteful experience to bring glory to God.

I encourage you to look at your pain from a different viewpoint. A right perspective can make all the difference in the world. Take a look at how you can use your pain for someone else's gain. Can your mess become your ministry? Maybe you have gone through so much that you feel you have enough experience to be a specialist in some area. I am a specialist in overcoming shame, guilt, poor self-image, lack of confidence, fear, anger, bitterness, self-pity, et cetera. Press past your pain and get your "master's degree" so you can work in the kingdom of restoring hurting people.[15]

To God's glory, that advice has brought this book to you. Maybe your story will lead you to a future of comforting others.

In the next chapter we will consider what this darkness looks like in the lives of three ministry wives who have met God in their depression.

■ FOR YOUR CONSIDERATION

1. Have you known anyone who has been through clinical depression?
2. Did you recognize the symptoms?
3. What are things you should and should not say to someone who is living with depression?
4. What are things you can do to help someone suffering through depression? Parker Palmer had a Quaker friend who came and washed his feet. To Palmer, this simple act reached beyond words and intentions and comforted him.
5. Can you identify with any of the stories in this chapter? If so, in what ways?

ELEVEN

Three Stories of Hope

Each of the following stories was shared with me by a godly, gracious ministry wife for your encouragement.

Carol (a pseudonym) hurried out to the car one spring evening intent on getting to her meeting on time. As she slid into the driver's seat, her mind was occupied with thoughts of her day at work, the dinner she had just had with her husband, the final draft of his seminary dissertation, and the looming student debt that would haunt them for years to come. She was full of hope for a successful future for their ministry. Her husband was talented, bright, committed to God, and she was one hundred percent in support of him, willing to sacrifice for his success. She drove into the parking lot of the seminary and scurried into the well-lit conference room where twenty or so seminary wives met to hear the "experts" give advice to ministry wives. The evening talk was full of recommendations on how to entertain guests, visiting missionaries, or church leaders. "Be sure your table linens are fresh, the dishes match, the corners of your living room and all flat surfaces are dust-free," concluded the expert.

This speaker joined the long list of women whose strengths Carol was intent on imitating. She was learning what a perfect ministry wife should be and was fully intent on becoming that person. Her husband and his ministry would thrive. If she could just get it right, she was certain that life would be kind, her husband would contribute meaningfully to the kingdom work, and she would gather her rewards from his successes.

He graduated, and they were called to their first assignment—a church that had seen great days of growth and impact in the past but was now declining. It was the intent of the district leaders that this would be the last attempt to resurrect the church. If her husband could not make a go of it, the church would close. She felt the pressure in her mind, but in her heart she was hopeful. They were ready, God was able, and life was calling.

For the first year or so, she poured herself into every perceived need of the church. She entertained guests almost continually for the first ten months, cleaning and cooking and succumbing to the whims of every perceived need she could address. It was exhausting. Slowly, but with withering certainty, she began to understand that she was failing at being the perfect parsonage wife she had set out to be. There were far too many needs in each day. There was an unlimited pile of tasks to be done with a limited supply of energy, mental facility, and emotional stamina. As she slogged away in an attempt to be all and do all, she lost the joy of the tasks.

The veneer of happiness remained resolutely in place, but in her heart there was a tear and slowly leaking from it were the dreams of her early days as a ministry wife. She was becoming more and more convinced that she was failing miserably at the single job she wanted so much to get right. She didn't dare mention her worries to her husband, because he had his own pressures to attend to, and she was certain she didn't want to deter him from his efforts to retool the struggling church. She plodded forward, weeping in the night when she reviewed the failures of the day. She always came to the same conclusion: the only way to get relief from the exhausting pain was to end her life.

It was unheard of that a pastor's wife should go to a counselor or even mention her heartache to anyone in the church. It remained hidden, increasing its stifling pressure.

The exhaustion of remaining outwardly intact while feeling inwardly as if she would explode was overwhelming. She contemplated how she could commit suicide in such a way that it would appear to be an accident. If she overdosed on sleeping pills it would be obvious and would mark the end of her husband's ministry. She couldn't do that to him. After weeks of twisted thoughts, she devised a plan. She would take the tan Volkswagen they owned and drive it off a high and deadly cliff. Ironically, she cried out to God, in whom she had little trust, to spare her from living with the paralysis that might occur in the aftermath of a failed attempt. What she needed more than anything was to successfully end her life. She had prayed and felt the prayers slapping her face with irony. She read her Bible but sensed only failure and guilt for not living up to its standards.

Finally, one cool September afternoon, after three nights of total emotional emptiness, she decided this would be the day. She was angry with God—if He even existed, with the people she blamed for her depression, with her husband, and the world. She clutched her jangling keys, surveyed the large, dustless parsonage she would never see again, and headed out to take the Volkswagen on its last journey.

When she told me her story, she clearly emphasized three things. First, she was thankful for her experience, difficult as it was to endure. She has gained an understanding of God and His love that has carried her through many subsequent struggles. She has been used by God to help others in similar situations, and for this she is truly grateful.

Second, she understands now that she was naive, insecure, and lacking in spiritual maturity. She had been resting on the assumption that doing the right thing was the most important part of her spiritual walk and that being the unique gift to the world that God intended was a distant second. Her walk with God was filled with what she should and shouldn't do rather than knowledge of or interest in the sweet presence of God.

Third, God is faithful. He was there all along, prodding, covering her with His wings, waiting for her to acknowledge and surrender her turmoil to Him. At this point in her story she began to convey this side of the narrative, the side where God was at work.

As she reached for the doorknob, the phone rang. It was her mother. "I just had an overwhelming impression that I should call you. How are you doing?"

"I just don't think I can do this pastor's wife thing anymore. It's far more difficult than I expected. I just can't keep going." She was not entirely honest about her plans, but the conversation was enough to keep her from proceeding out to the garage. When her husband came home that evening, she gave him this ultimatum. "If you want this marriage to last, you need to get out of the ministry."

Shocked, he asked if he might have some time to close down the work he was doing and transition away from the church. "I'll give you some time," she responded without enthusiasm.

They talked and prayed until the sun shed its pink shades across the sky. She questioned her husband about what it meant to be sanctified—or set apart—as it is described in the New Testament. Her concept of this doctrine demanded that she be perfect, never angry, never ill-tempered, never self-centered, and she could not live up to it. She discovered, and this was one of the turning points of her life, that it meant to be truly given over to God, to place at His feet her baggage, anger, hurts, naiveté, wounds, and all.

Somehow, during that long night of conversation, in some enigmatic way, God revealed himself to her, and she knew He was there. From that point on, she never entertained suicidal thoughts again, even though depression has surged repeatedly.

She spilled all the heartache into the space between her and her husband and let him share the caustic overflow and draw close. They slept for a couple of hours and rose to face another day.

By ten that morning she felt nothing. Nada. Empty. She was inexpressibly angry at God. *So this is the way you tricked me, God! This is how you work. You are forcing me to choose to survive by trusting in you alone. No reassurance, no feelings of relief, only demanding that I trust in the absence of all feeling. I will make this bargain: I'll try this for three months, and if I don't commit suicide, I'll renew this contract at that time.*

For a year and a half, she lived three months at a time, renewing the contract on each expiration date. She said, "Honestly, I never once had further suicidal thoughts."

That initial contract was her surrender. It was what God was looking for all along.

God was at work, slowly pulling the thin threads of her soul to himself. In quiet, certain love He brought healing, He answered her prayer for the reconciling of three relationships in the church. Women she had hated were brought under that surrender, and consequently God placed love in her heart that enveloped even them. He gave her the strength to stand by her dying mother-in-law who lay in the hospital, a place she avoided at all cost. For five days she ministered to her husband's mother and felt the comfort of God's Spirit. She watched as God stepped in to prevent a decision to move that she knew she could not endure. Her unspoken paradigm became "Don't let me miss what God may have to teach me."

She understood the healing that had taken place on a warm, tropical evening when a very influential woman came to her house for dinner. The woman was not satisfied with parts of the meal she had prepared, and after their company left, she turned to her husband and said, "That's her problem!" They laughed together, and she felt the wings of her soul unfold.

One final message she wanted me to relay began with an incident that occurred a few years back, sometime after her days of depression. She and her husband had been experiencing some difficulties—the death of a close family member, a recurrence of breast cancer, and some very pressing legal issues when she decided to talk to her doctor about the possibility of using antidepressants to help her cope with the pain of the crushing, unrelenting pressure. Under his advice, and with some reluctance and guilt, she began a short course of antidepressant medication.

In her search for temporary relief one weekend, she and her husband decided to attend a Bill Gaither concert in a distant city. While there she bought a CD set of Dr. Archibald Hart's titled "The Christian and Depression."

On the way home they listened to the Christian professor, speaker, and author address the subject of depression. He suggested that for many people changing the biochemistry of the brain so that it functioned in a more normal range was an appropriate response to a biochemical problem. He encouraged his listeners to understand that antidepressant medication was a perfectly acceptable option for advancing their mental health.

"It was so liberating to hear him say that. I felt as if a load of guilt was lifted from my shoulders. Medicine is OK. I had had so much heartache and trauma that year that I needed it. I no longer felt ashamed to get the help I required. I had permission to take this step toward wholeness."

God is faithful. He is behind the scenes willing you to surrender your pain to Him, to find Jesus in the flesh through godly counselors and sound, medical advice. He is waiting for you to give Him your childhood God in exchange for a loving God who softly whispers, *I am with you, always.*

✳ ✳ ✳

Karen (not her real name) and her husband were well into their eighth year of ministry when it struck. There was evidence of it earlier, like fingers lightly touching her heart. Not enough to interrupt the daily rhythms of her life, but certainly there in quiet persistence. Fear, once a subtle enemy, struck after the birth of her first child, who had been anticipated with great joy. Karen had been told that pregnancy for her was very unlikely. The paralyzing anxiety gripping her heart tightened and began to interfere with the smooth cadence of her life. Filled with both pride and anxiety, she brought the baby to church the first

Sunday and wouldn't allow anyone to lift her from the baby carrier for fear that disease germs on their hands would make the baby sick. She didn't put the baby in the nursery, and she didn't want anyone to hold her.

The gripping fear that some misfortune would strike spilled over into other areas of her life. The task of driving in the southern, metropolitan city in which she lived became fraught with so much apprehension that she found her world shrinking until leaving the house became a dread. Traveling on overpasses sent waves of adrenalin through her tense body. She remembers a long line of traffic backed up behind her car as she tried to drive onto an overpass. The constriction around her heart pressed and strengthened, shutting off the joy of living.

It culminated when she was elected to a position in her denomination's statewide conference that required her to travel to a meeting, eat a meal in a hotel, organize a large group of women, then return home. She stood at the front door of her home as she prepared to leave, staring with focused anxiety at the car in the driveway waiting to take her to the meeting. Her face was drawn in fretful lines as she considered the roads that would be impossibly dangerous, the overpasses that were sure to collapse and smash into the traffic below. There were germs in the food at the hotel and on the hands of people who were careless about washing them. She could not do this thing. It was beyond her.

Conflicted, she convinced her husband to drive her to the hotel. Once there, she sat in the car and wept for some time while her husband prayed that she could leave the car, eat what was placed before her, and carry on the business ahead. She came to understand that these acute experiences were known as panic attacks.

Fearing more the failure she would become if this simple meeting could not be conquered, she dried her eyes, checked her makeup, tucked a strand of black hair into place, and opened the car door. Through God in His grace, she completed all that was necessary and concealed from all but her husband the tumult of her experience.

When she was relaying this to me, her voice broke, and the words crumpled out in starts and stops. "This is painful for you, isn't it?" I asked gently.

"It's such a miracle when I look back on it. Even then, before He brought me real healing, He was chiseling away at my fears. Now, almost every time I sit behind the wheel of my car, I praise God for His faithfulness. I was driving the other night, enjoying a degree of freedom I only dreamed was possible, going seventy miles per hour just praising God that I could drive without fear," she responded.

"How did this healing come about?"

She said there came a time on a sunny August afternoon when the worst of these phobias were pried from her heart and cast into the sea of past shame, forgiven, and healed, not to return in their all-possessing form again.

She had returned from a successful retreat, and because she was in the process of recovering from a hysterectomy, she had temporarily released all her church and district responsibilities. She sat leaning back in her recliner praising the Lord for His graces in her life, her Bible open on her lap. In the quiet of that afternoon alone with God, her mind drifted over the verse that began a conversation with God and would take her to a genuine release from these gripping fears.

It was as though she heard "'Come now, let us reason together,' says the LORD. 'Though your sins are like scarlet, they shall be as white as snow; though they are red as crimson, they shall be like wool'" (Isaiah 1:18). Slowly, and with great precision, the Great Physician began to peel away the layers of perfectionism, fear, jealousy, self-centeredness, and egocentrism. At each layer, she prayed for understanding and forgiveness, and the next layer would surface.

The room was filled with gentle light, and in the center of all, she felt the great love of the Divine as she went through layer upon layer of troubling past events. She understood that her childhood had been surrounded by expectations imposed by a perfectionist mother, that God was the only one she needed to please, and when He was pleased everything else was far less important.

She saw that the anger she felt toward her husband, who was gone so much of the time that she often felt like a single parent, needed to be confessed. She saw that instead of embracing him upon his return home each day, she chastised him, which only made his coming home more uncomfortable. He had to be released to serve without the guilt she tried to impose on him.

She released the need to control her environment and her need to protect members of her family and keep them free from germs, accidents, and pain. She looked up the many types of fear mentioned in the Scriptures and understood that she was consumed by situational fears—the kind that stopped her from driving or eating out. These were the fears she had to face in her world.

It was embarrassing, and she could not admit her fears to anyone. She suffered from ego fears, including the fear of looking like a failure in the eyes of others, of being thought of as incapable. God showed her that she had been focusing on herself and all she loved and that this was a form of idolatry. She understood her pretense and released the things she clutched to her heart in the presence of this great love, this sanctifying power.

"Since that time, have these fears ever returned?" I asked.

"I have had to surrender small, sometimes growing buds of fear again and again, but the process gets easier because I can see that God can be trusted to bring healing as I face them. It used to be daily, now it is just occasionally. I consider myself to have normal fears that keep a person from doing foolish things, but fear no longer possesses me. I am emotionally healthy by the power of God's Spirit." Her voice broke and joy spread into her eyes and into the lines of her face as she wept once more.

I asked what her advice would be to others suffering as she did. What follows is her answer:

First, if you are struggling with fear, talk to your doctor or a professional Christian counselor. Make this a top priority. Find the money and do it.

You may be overstimulated with mountainous activity, emotions, or thoughts, or as she was, you may be insecure, jealous of your husband's time and interest, and self-centered. These may be overpowering your ability to manage your fear or your life. You may feel as if you are in a spiritual wilderness and unable to find joy or interest in the things of God. These emotions bind your heart and keep it from allowing the free flow of God's love to your family and the world around you.

You can admit them to God, repent of them, and feel His immense love in your surrender. Give them to the God who made you, knows you, and loves you beyond measure. You are His treasure. You can trust Him with everything. Let Him breathe love into each relationship. You can serve your family and God from a heart of love rather than duty or expectation. Operating in your own strength and determination to do everything right is a recipe for frustration in ministry.

Second, know that there is strength in the name and in the words of the Lord. Use His name in praise for what healing He will bring, is bringing, or has brought. God's Word is paramount. It was not until I saturated myself with God's Word and understood how to apply it that I found the strength for overcoming. I memorized scripture so that when any wave of anxiety came, I began to praise God.

Third, if you are trying to live in your own strength and without the power of God, there will be others affected by your lifestyle. Your children will develop some of the habits you illustrate for them. The impact of these habits on others is the price you pay for keeping the fears in your heart. Release them to God and let Him bring His love and power into your life. This is not a simple task; it will take time, grace, persistence, faith, and honesty, but God has power and grace to give you if you start.

Be comforted; God is able.

"I sought the Lord, and he answered me; he delivered me from all my fears" (Psalm 34:4).

* * *

Linda (not her real name) sat on the white, sparkling Caribbean beach as the tropical sun spread warmth across her shoulders down to her feet. The light breeze set shallow ruffled waves lapping at the shoreline. In her hand was her Bible. She had come to worship God in the quiet blue of the afternoon. She listened with almost mesmerizing concentration to the rhythmic shush, shush of the waves as they rose and fell, rose and fell into shining flat blades across the beach. She thought she understood how Jesus might love the Sea of Galilee with its sounds, sparkling waves, and tiny boats perched along its rustic shoreline.

Quietly she sat and waited, picturing this sea of the New Testament. From the corner of her vision she sensed more than saw a shadow moving across the sand, darkening then clearing the uneven surface as it moved. She held her breath and in quiet, gentle sounds as soft as the whisper of the breeze she heard, *I love you. You are precious to me. You are of immeasurable value to me.* She exhaled softly and reveled in the sweet knowledge of God's approval.

These words were to sustain her in a time of coming turmoil, the likes of which she could not have imagined in that moment on the beach. They drew around her heart like a lovely, soft shawl, covered her soul with assurance, and gave her peace.

Like most ministry wives young in the service of God, she had dreams of helping people, of fixing broken hearts, patching the holes in torn relationships, healing the aches of troubled children, and ministering to the needs of the elderly. She readily admits now that she is a recovering enabler, codependent on those she serves, and that she had spent much of her early years naive and ill-equipped to understand her limitations. She was convinced that God expected her to be entirely selfless, to put others first, to deny herself and give without expecting anything in return. I suspect that's the way many of us start out.

Life became complex as life does for all of us. Slowly, but with increasing intensity, problems collected. Each congregant and family problem that shadowed her pathway felt like a personal responsibility, hers alone to solve.

She could not discuss her distress with her husband, because his early childhood had brought him to understand that one did not speak of such personal problems. They were not to be taken out or displayed and discussed. Just suck it up, he thought. As she lost more and more spiritual and emotional reserve, the weight of the unresolved dilemmas was enormous and came crashing down on a bright September day. So much had contributed to the collapse.

She lived with her husband and family in a tiny house near an intersection where drugs were routinely bought and sold, where there had been the recent shooting of a young man, where danger lingered like early morning fog on each corner. She was trying to meet the transportation, emotional, and physical needs of an elderly friend. The two foster children she was caring for required therapeutic intervention.

Her son, who was suicidal and struggling with a drug addiction, was living with them attempting to find help. The word on the street was that this son had incurred the wrath of a local drug outfit and was in danger of the same fate as the young man shot down on the street corner. She was terrified for his life, and the emotional strain of it clawed at her heart each waking moment.

Because he was a pastor, her husband refused to entertain the thought of counseling, though she begged for it. He *gave* counseling, he did not *receive* it. Every aspect of her life was fraught with the stress of serious and unresolved problems. It was up to her to fix things, and she no longer had the resources or strength to consider any solutions, so the unresolved pile grew higher and higher.

The final weight that sent the whole stack crashing down came one morning as she was trying to help her son attend a

Bible study for recovering addicts. His frustration and anger foamed and exploded. She was the nearest target, so he spewed on her his rage and exasperation. This is a normal thing for people in his position, she later learned, but that morning it was the final revelation of her helplessness to fix the problem. She had tried so hard to be all that everyone needed her to be, to fix the problems she encountered. The effort had become excruciatingly difficult.

She could no longer handle life as she was now experiencing it. Her hazel eyes clouded with the mistaken idea that everyone would be happier if she would just go away forever. Weeping, she threw open the front door and broke free of the neighborhood on her way to a wooded area near her home. Blinded by tears, considering suicide—or at the very least not ever returning—she stumbled up into a tree-shaded forest, away from the marked trail in an attempt to find a secluded place to cry alone.

At this point in the interview, she pauses to allow the tears to ease down her cheeks.

"Is this painful for you?" I ask.

"I don't go back there very often. It still hurts to remember," she responds.

She wipes her eyes, sniffles a bit, and continues.

She came upon a small, shaded clearing in the woods some distance from the trail and sat down on a brown log to cry. She cried for a long time, calling out to God to help her son make it through the day. She so feared for his life and for her own sanity that she lost track of the hours that passed.

The afternoon sun warmed the air, and in a moment of quiet between sobs, she heard the snap of breaking twigs. She was mortified that someone might find her in this condition, and since she was some distance from the trail she thought it unlikely. The sounds continued until someone came close and stopped. She refused to look up or acknowledge the person who stood before her.

"Can we help you? Please, can we do something for you?" It was the voice of a woman who spoke with kind and caring words.

She shook her head even as the woman continued imploring. She continued to shake her head, refusing to look into the faces of this woman and her husband.

Finally the husband spoke. "I am a minister, and I think I can help you." She grimaced and thought, *Yea, right! I have had enough of those for quite a while.* Still she shook her head.

He continued. "I have been going through a lot of issues in my own life and have found a good counselor that I would like for you to consider. I have his card and will leave it here with you. Please, consider going." He reached down and handed her the card. During this entire interchange she never looked up or saw the faces of these caring people. They left and walked down the hill back to the trail.

God had begun His rescue through these people. His attempts to teach her that she was not responsible for the healing of all who hurt were met with confused denial until there were no personal resources left and she had only Him to call to. In a real sense His whisper to her was, *Now, I have begun to hear and answer your cry for help. Are you ready to listen?*

She sat on the log for some time longer, and as the sun lowered into gray coolness she descended from the high place and went home.

She placed the card before her husband that evening and said to him, "Call this number, or I won't be around for you to do it. I can't take any more, and if you don't get some help for me I am going to go away—forever."

He could see from the set of her face that he could not ignore her words, so he called the number on the card. Yes, the counselor could take her right now. Yes, he was personally affiliated with a Christian church. Yes, please, both of you come in to talk.

This first time with a counselor was very difficult for her husband who was still reluctant to open his heart to anyone. The counselor listened thoughtfully, asked questions to clarify, and gave her an assignment for the coming week. "You must do something for yourself this week and report to me what you have done when you come back next week."

She had no idea what he meant, and it took her many days to understand what he was asking her to do. It had been so long since she had done anything for herself or even thought of what that might be that the concept was as foreign as a book written in another language. After much consideration, she settled on a plan to get a massage at a local spa. She lay on the massage table and wept the whole time as she released the tensions of many years and much trouble.

God began to help her pick up the pieces of her broken reality and develop a new lifestyle, a new way of thinking about her own resources and responsibilities. Each week she had to do something for herself and report the activity to her counselor.

She pauses here in the interview, collects her thoughts, and draws a conclusion worth repeating: There is a fine line that must be understood between being selfless and being a good steward of oneself. It is a boundary, though sometimes shifting, that must be clear and solid. A book that has helped her to understand this is *The Lies We Believe* by Dr. Chris Thurman.

Her counselor had her go through this book and its workbook when they met. This and the grace of God have brought her slowly back from an intolerable lifestyle.

God's answers were just beginning with the events at the clearing in the woods.

After some time of seeing her son continue in his destructive ways, knowing his life was in danger, she was given the name of a judge in town that she thought might be sympathetic to her fears. This judge suggested that she bring her son in to his county judicial chambers to be assessed. She had no idea how to get him there. Her son was, at this point, very uncooperative. So she gave the judge the address of the place where she thought her son might be.

Early one morning soon after, the local police were sent on a drug raid to the apartment where they found her son with some drugs in his possession. He was awakened by the stern voice of a policeman who held a pistol to his head and ordered, "Don't move." Her son was arrested, jailed, and the judge called and told her that her son was safely locked up and would not be in mortal danger. His sentence was either one year in jail or a stint at Teen Challenge. He chose the latter.

"He is my miracle son." Her voice breaks as she continues. "He is a changed man. He has given his life to Christ and now years later he is serving in the church, is a functioning member of society, and loves God. God heard my cry for help and has given me a new life. I have a wonderful support group that meets regularly at our church. It provides me with a ministry and with help for myself."

She is truly a new creation. Her face is a reflection of the joy that comes from a deep central reservoir of grace that she allows God to fill regularly. She has learned how to say no when it is necessary, and she is eternally grateful for God's assurance that He is listening.

* * *

May these stories provide you with hope that God is at work in your darkest times. He *is* faithful.

With continuous prayers for your victory in Christ,
Donna

Notes

Chapter 1

1. William P. Brown, *Character in Crisis: A Fresh Approach to the Wisdom Literature of the Old Testament* (Grand Rapids, Mich.: Eerdmans, 1996).

Chapter 2

1. Donna B. Alder, *Pastors' Wives Study* (Lenexa, Kans.: Presentation to SDMI Advisory Committee of the Church of the Nazarene, February 2009).

2. Duane P. Alleman, *The Psychosocial Adjustment of Pastors' Wives* (Doctoral dissertation, Fuller Theological Seminary, 1987).

3. Sandi Brunette-Hill, "A Life of Her Own: Role Change Among Clergy Wives," in *Social Scientific Study of Religion* 10 (1999): 77-90.

4. Kenneth E. Crow, *Executive Summary: Task Force on the Family Survey of Ministers' Wives* (Report of the National Association of Evangelicals Task Force on the Family, 1990), data charts, 1-44.

5. William Douglas, *Ministers' Wives* (New York: Harper and Row, 1965).

6. M. Taylor, S. Hartley, and S. Foster, "Two Person Career: A Classic Example," in *Sociology of Work and Occupations*, 2(4) (November 1975): 64-69.

7. Pat Valeriano, "A Survey of Ministers' Wives," in *Leadership Journal* 2(4) (Fall 1981): 64-69.

Chapter 3

1. Donna B. Alder, *Help, I'm a Pastor's Wife* (Orlando, Fla.: Presentation to SSDMI workshop at the General Assembly of the Church of the Nazarene, June 2009).

2. John Piper, *What Jesus Demands from the World* (Wheaton, Ill.: Crossway Books, 2006), 83-91.

3. C. S. Lewis, *The Weight of Glory, and Other Addresses* (Grand Rapids, Mich.: Eerdmans, 1965), 2.

4. Piper, *What Jesus Demands,* 85.

Chapter 4

1. Jeffrey Young, *Schema Therapy: Early Maladaptive Schemas and Schema Domains* (2003), http://www.schematherapy.com/id73.htm.

2. David M. Dunkley, David C. Zuroff, Kirk R. Blankstein, "Specific Perfectionism Components Versus Self-Criticism in Predicting Maladjustment," in *Personality and Individual Differences*, 40 (2006).

3. Anne Wilson Schaef, *When Society Becomes an Addict* (San Francisco: Harper and Row, 1987), 68.

4. Melinda Beck, "Silencing the Voice That Says You're a Fraud," in the *Wall Street Journal* (June 16, 2009). http://online.wsj.com/article/SB124511712673817527.html.

5. Joyce Meyer, *Eat the Cookie. . . Buy the Shoes: Giving Yourself Permission to Lighten Up* (New York: Faith Words, 2010), 128.

6. Ibid., 77.

7. Ibid., 25.

8. Barbra Goodyear Minar, *Unrealistic Expectations* (Wheaton, Ill.: Victor Books, 1990), 66.

9. http://pastoralcareinc.com/WhyPastoralCare/Statistics.php. Pastoral Care, Inc. Statistics provided by the Fuller Institute, George Barna, and Pastoral Care, Inc.

10. Robert I. Ayling, *The Role Anticipations of Student Ministers' Wives* (Boston: Boston School of Theology, Unpublished doctoral dissertation, 1964), 217.

Chapter 5

1. Joyce Meyer, *Approval Addiction: Overcoming Your Need to Please Everyone* (New York: Warner Faith, 2005), 97.

2. H. B. London and Neil Wiseman, *Married to a Pastor: How to Stay Happily Married in the Ministry* (Ventura, Calif.: Regal, 1999), 124.

3. Ibid., 125.

4. Meyer, *Approval Addiction,* 14-15.

5. Teresa Flint-Borden with Barbara Cooper, *Women Married to Men in Ministry: Breaking the Sound Barrier Together* (Nashville: Abingdon, 2007), 112.

6. Crow, K (1990, February). *National Association of Evangelicals Task Force on the Family Survey of Ministers' Wives: Executive Summary.* Unpublished manuscript. See p. 1-43.

7. Meyer, *Approval Addiction,* 5.

8. William Douglas, *Ministers' Wives* (New York: Harper and Row, 1965), 187.

Chapter 6

1. Wendy Murray Zoba, "What Pastors' Wives Wish Their Churches Knew," *Christianity Today* 41(4) (1997), 20-26. P. 5.

2. Pat Valeriano, "A Survey of Ministers' Wives," in *Leadership Journal* 2(4) (Fall 1981): 64-69.

3. Mary LaGrand Bouma, "Ministers' Wives: The Walking Wounded," in *Leadership Journal* 1(1) (Winter 1980): 63-75. P. 67.

4. Sandi Brunette-Hill, "A Life of Her Own: Role Change Among Clergy Wives," in *Social Scientific Study of Religion* 10 (1999): 77-90, p. 81.

5. W. Crow, *National Association of Evangelicals Task Force on the Family Survey of Ministers' Wives: Executive Summary.* Unpublished manuscript (February 1990), see pp. 1-44.

6. Duane P. Alleman, *The Psychosocial Adjustment of Pastors' Wives* (Pasadena, Calif.: Fuller Theological Seminary, Unpublished doctoral dissertation, 1987), 87-90.

7. Douglas, *Ministers' Wives,* 229-39.

8. Crow, K. (1990, February). *National Association of Evangelicals Task Force on the Family Survey of Ministers' Wives: Executive Summary.* Unpublished manuscript. See p. 1-43.

9. Douglas, *Ministers' Wives,* 236.

10. Alleman, *Psychosocial Adjustment of Pastors' Wives,* 45.

11. Roy M. Oswald, *Why Do Clergy Wives Burn Out? Action Information of the Alban Institute* 10(2) (Herndon, Va.: Alban Institute, 1984), 1-5.

12. London and Wiseman, *Married to a Pastor,* 186.

13. Lorna Dobson, *I'm More than a Pastor's Wife: Authentic Living in a Fishbowl World* (Grand Rapids, Mich.: Zondervan, 2003), 86-87.

14. Ruth Senter, *The Guilt-Free Book for Pastors' Wives* (Wheaton, Ill.: Victor Books, 1990), 99.

15. Meyer, *Approval Addiction,* 123.

16. Elizabeth Gilbert, *Committed: A Skeptic Makes Peace with Marriage* (New York: Random House, 2010), see chapter 2.

17. Crow, K. (1990, February). *National Association of Evangelicals Task Force on the Family Survey of Ministers' Wives: Executive summary.* Unpublished manuscript. See p. 1-43.

18. Carol Kent, *Secret Passions of the Christian Woman* (Colorado Springs: NavPress, 1990), 121.

19. Paul Tournier, *Creative Suffering* (San Francisco: Harper and Row, 1983), 52.

20. London and Wiseman, *Married to a Pastor,* 190-91.

21. Thomas J. Oord and Michael Lodahl, *Relational Holiness: Responding to the Call of Love* (Kansas City: Beacon Hill Press of Kansas City, 2005).

22. Valeriano, "Survey of Ministers' Wives," 67.

23. Susie Hawkins, *From One Ministry Wife to Another: Honest Conversations About Ministry Connections* (Chicago: Moody Publishers, 2009), 75.

24. Joyce Williams, ed., *She Can't Even Play the Piano: Insights for Ministry Wives* (Kansas City: Beacon Hill Press of Kansas City, 2005), 75.

25. Michele Buckingham, ed., *Help! I'm a Pastor's Wife* (Altamonte Springs, Fla.: Creation Press, 1986).

26. Gayle Haggard, *A Life Embraced: A Hopeful Guide for the Pastor's Wife* (Colorado Springs: WaterBrook Press, 2005), chapter 8.

27. Jill Briscoe, *Renewal on the Run: Embracing the Privileges and Expectations of a Ministry Wife* (Birmingham, Ala.: New Hope Publishers, 2005), 28.

28. Williams, *She Can't Even Play the Piano,* 77.

29. Kent, *Secret Passions of the Christian Woman,* 110-14.

30. Elisabeth Elliot, *Loneliness* (Nashville: Oliver-Nelson, 1988), back cover.

Chapter 7

1. Cdsblessed, "Thinking about leaving pastor husband" (online forum comment). Retrieved from www.focusonlinecommunities.com/message/42429 (October 31, 2007).

2. Oswald, "Why Do Clergy Wives Burn Out?" 1-5.

3. Alleman, *Psychosocial Adjustment of Pastors' Wives,* 40.

4. Ibid., 98.

5. Ibid., 38.

6. Crow, *Survey of Ministers' Wives: Executive Summary,* 1-44.

7. David Congo and Janet Congo, *Free to Soar* (Old Tappan, N.J.: Fleming H. Revell, 1987), 62-63.

8. Dobson, *I'm More than a Pastor's Wife,* 148-50.

9. Martie Stowell, "When He Doesn't Keep His Promises," chapter 11 in *The Joy of a Promise Kept: The Powerful Role Wives Play* (Sisters, Oreg.: Multnomah Books, 1996), 168.

Chapter 8

1. A. W. Tozer, *The Knowledge of the Holy* (New York: Harper and Row, 1961), 121.

2. Douglas, *Ministers' Wives,* 234.

3. Dallas Willard, *The Spirit of the Disciplines* (San Francisco: Harper and Row, 1988).

4. Richard Foster, *Celebration of Discipline: The Path to Spiritual Growth,* rev. ed. (San Francisco: Harper San Francisco, 1988).

5. Crow, *Survey of Ministers' Wives: Executive Summary,* 1-44.

6. Douglas, *Ministers' Wives,* 78-80.

7. Gordon MacDonald, *Ordering Your Private World* (Nashville: Thomas Nelson, 2003), see chapters 11—14.

8. Ibid., 151.

9. Mother Teresa, *A Gift for God: Prayers and Meditations* (New York: HarperCollins, 1996), 68.

10. MacDonald, *Ordering Your Private World,* 153.

11. Williams, *She Can't Even Play the Piano,* 11.

12. MacDonald, *Ordering Your Private World,* see chapter 12.

13. Foster, *Celebration of Discipline,* 15.

14. Ibid., 20.

15. Ibid., 24-25.

16. Williams, *She Can't Even Play the Piano,* 122-23.

17. Ibid., 124.

18. Charles Swindoll, *So You Want to Be like Christ? Eight Essentials to Get You There* (Nashville: W Publishing Group of Thomas Nelson, 2005), 126.

19. Andrew Murray, *Humility* (New Kensington, Pa.: Whitaker House, 1982), 75.

Chapter 9

1. Douglas, *Ministers' Wives,* 127-28.

2. Ibid., 187.

3. Ibid., 191.

4. Crow, *Survey of Ministers' Wives: Executive Summary,* 14.

5. Ibid., 31-35.

6. T. T. Hsieh, E. F. Rugg, "Coping Patterns of Ministers' Wives," in *Journal of Psychology and Christianity* 2(3) (1984): 73.

7. Valeriano, "Survey of Ministers' Wives," 71.

8. Stephen R. Covey, *7 Habits of Highly Effective People* (New York: Simon and Schuster, 1989), see chapter 7.

9. Oswald, "Why Do Clergy Wives Burn Out?" 3-4.

10. Senter, *Guilt-Free Book for Pastors' Wives,* see chapter 5.

11. Zoba, "What Pastors' Wives Wish Their Churches Knew," 20-26.

12. London and Wiseman, *Married to a Pastor,* see chapter 10.

13. Ibid., 256-73.

14. Ibid.

15. Mother Teresa, Mother Teresa of Calcutta speaks on priesthood. Retrieved from http://www.clerus.org/clerus/dati/2010-04/20-13/Mother_Teresa_to_the_priests.pdf (n.d.).

Chapter 10

1. Lynn Hybels, *Nice Girls Don't Change the World* (Grand Rapids, Mich.: Zondervan, 2005), 28, 31, 36.

2. Sue Monk Kidd, *Firstlight* (New York: Guideposts Books, 2006), 14.

3. Ibid., 16.

4. *Types of Depression: Definitions and Terminology.* Retrieved from http://www.depression-help-resource.com/types-of-depression.htm.

5. L. S. Mintle, *Breaking Free from Depression* (Lake Mary, Fla.: Charisma House, 2002).

6. J. Larson, *Alcoholism: The Biochemical Connection.* Retrieved from http://www.trans4mind.com/nutrition/depression.html (n.d.).

7. Mintle, *Breaking Free from Depression*, 2-4.

8. David Currie, "Escaping the Swamp of Depression," in *Leadership Journal* (Winter 1992): 100-104.

9. Mintle, *Breaking Free from Depression.*

10. Joyce Meyer, *Seven Things That Steal Your Joy: Overcoming the Obstacles to Your Happiness* (New York: FaithWords, 2005).

11. Archibald Hart and Catherine Hart Weber, *Unveiling Depression in Women: A Practical Guide to Understanding and Overcoming Depression* (Old Tappan, N.J.: Fleming H. Revell, 2002).

12. S. Baldauf, "If the Gloom Won't Lift," in *US News and World Report* 146(11) (December 2009): 72.

13. R. Middleton, lecture from "Wisdom Literature" class (September 4, 2008), Roberts Wesleyan College.

14. C. Tippett, producer, *The Soul in Depression* [Audio podcast]. Retrieved from http://being.publicradio.org/programs/depression/kristasjournal.shtml.

15. Meyer, *Approval Addiction*, 237.